W9-BTL-284

Nutshell Series

of

WEST PUBLISHING COMPANY

P.O. Box 64526

St. Paul, Minnesota 55164–0526

———

Accounting—Law and, 1984, 377 pages, by E. McGruder Faris, Late Professor of Law, Stetson University.

Administrative Law and Process, 2nd Ed., 1981, 445 pages, by Ernest Gellhorn, Dean and Professor of Law, Case Western Reserve University and Barry B. Boyer, Professor of Law, SUNY, Buffalo.

Admiralty, 1983, 390 pages, by Frank L. Maraist, Professor of Law, Louisiana State University.

Agency-Partnership, 1977, 364 pages, by Roscoe T. Steffen, Late Professor of Law, University of Chicago.

American Indian Law, 1981, 288 pages, by William C. Canby, Jr., Adjunct Professor of Law, Arizona State University.

Antitrust Law and Economics, 2nd Ed., 1981, 425 pages, by Ernest Gellhorn, Dean and Professor of Law, Case Western Reserve University.

Appellate Advocacy, 1984, 325 pages, by Alan D. Hornstein, Professor of Law, University of Maryland.

Art Law, 1984, 335 pages, by Leonard D. DuBoff, Professor of Law, Lewis and Clark College, Northwestern School of Law.

Banking and Financial Institutions, 1984, 409 pages, by William A. Lovett, Professor of Law, Tulane University.

Church-State Relations—Law of, 1981, 305 pages, by Leonard F. Manning, Late Professor of Law, Fordham University.

Civil Procedure, 1979, 271 pages, by Mary Kay Kane, Professor of Law, University of California, Hastings College of the Law.

Civil Rights, 1978, 279 pages, by Norman Vieira, Professor of Law, Southern Illinois University.

Commercial Paper, 3rd Ed., 1982, 404 pages, by Charles M. Weber, Professor of Business Law, University of Arizona and Richard E. Speidel, Professor of Law, Northwestern University.

Community Property, 1982, 423 pages, by Robert L. Mennell, Former Professor of Law, Hamline University.

Comparative Legal Traditions, 1982, 402 pages, by Mary Ann Glendon, Professor of Law, Boston College, Michael Wallace Gordon, Professor of Law, University of Florida and Christopher Osakwe, Professor of Law, Tulane University.

Conflicts, 1982, 469 pages, by David D. Siegel, Professor of Law, Albany Law School, Union University.

Constitutional Analysis, 1979, 388 pages, by Jerre S. Williams, Professor of Law Emeritus, University of Texas.

Constitutional Power—Federal and State, 1974, 411 pages, by David E. Engdahl, Professor of Law, University of Puget Sound.

Consumer Law, 2nd Ed., 1981, 418 pages, by David G. Epstein, Professor of Law, University of Texas and Steve H. Nickles, Professor of Law, University of Minnesota.

Contract Remedies, 1981, 323 pages, by Jane M. Friedman, Professor of Law, Wayne State University.

Contracts, 2nd Ed., 1983, 425 pages, by Gordon D. Schaber, Dean and Professor of Law, McGeorge School of Law and Claude D. Rohwer, Professor of Law, McGeorge School of Law.

Corporations—Law of, 1980, 379 pages, by Robert W. Hamilton, Professor of Law, University of Texas.

Corrections and Prisoners' Rights—Law of, 2nd Ed., 1983, 384 pages, by Sheldon Krantz, Dean and Professor of Law, University of San Diego.

NUTSHELL SERIES

Criminal Law, 1975, 302 pages, by Arnold H. Loewy, Professor of Law, University of North Carolina.

Criminal Procedure—Constitutional Limitations, 3rd Ed., 1980, 438 pages, by Jerold H. Israel, Professor of Law, University of Michigan and Wayne R. LaFave, Professor of Law, University of Illinois.

Debtor-Creditor Law, 2nd Ed., 1980, 324 pages, by David G. Epstein, Professor of Law, University of Texas.

Employment Discrimination—Federal Law of, 2nd Ed., 1981, 402 pages, by Mack A. Player, Professor of Law, University of Georgia.

Energy Law, 1981, 338 pages, by Joseph P. Tomain, Professor of Law, University of Cincinnatti.

Environmental Law, 1983, 343 pages by Roger W. Findley, Professor of Law, University of Illinois and Daniel A. Farber, Professor of Law, University of Minnesota.

Estate Planning—Introduction to, 3rd Ed., 1983, 370 pages, by Robert J. Lynn, Professor of Law, Ohio State University.

Evidence, Federal Rules of, 1981, 428 pages, by Michael H. Graham, Professor of Law, University of Miami.

Evidence, State and Federal Rules, 2nd Ed., 1981, 514 pages, by Paul F. Rothstein, Professor of Law, Georgetown University.

Family Law, 1977, 400 pages, by Harry D. Krause, Professor of Law, University of Illinois.

Federal Estate and Gift Taxation, 3rd Ed., 1983, 509 pages, by John K. McNulty, Professor of Law, University of California, Berkeley.

Federal Income Taxation of Individuals, 3rd Ed., 1983, 487 pages, by John K. McNulty, Professor of Law, University of California, Berkeley.

Federal Income Taxation of Corporations and Stockholders, 2nd Ed., 1981, 362 pages, by Jonathan Sobeloff, Late Professor of Law, Georgetown University and Peter P. Weidenbruch, Jr., Professor of Law, Georgetown University.

Federal Jurisdiction, 2nd Ed., 1981, 258 pages, by David P. Currie, Professor of Law, University of Chicago.

Future Interests, 1981, 361 pages, by Lawrence W. Waggoner, Professor of Law, University of Michigan.

Government Contracts, 1979, 423 pages, by W. Noel Keyes, Professor of Law, Pepperdine University.

Historical Introduction to Anglo-American Law, 2nd Ed., 1973, 280 pages, by Frederick G. Kempin, Jr., Professor of Business Law, Wharton School of Finance and Commerce, University of Pennsylvania.

Immigration Law and Procedure, 1984, 345 pages, by David Weissbrodt, Professor of Law, University of Minnesota.

Injunctions, 1974, 264 pages, by John F. Dobbyn, Professor of Law, Villanova University.

Insurance Law, 1981, 281 pages, by John F. Dobbyn, Professor of Law, Villanova University.

Intellectual Property—Patents, Trademarks and Copyright, 1983, 428 pages, by Arthur R. Miller, Professor of Law, Harvard University, and Michael H. Davis, Professor of Law, Cleveland State University, Cleveland-Marshall College of Law.

International Business Transactions, 2nd Ed., 1984, 476 pages, by Donald T. Wilson, Professor of Law, Loyola University, Los Angeles.

Introduction to the Study and Practice of Law, 1983, 418 pages, by Kenney F. Hegland, Professor of Law, University of Arizona.

Judicial Process, 1980, 292 pages, by William L. Reynolds, Professor of Law, University of Maryland.

Jurisdiction, 4th Ed., 1980, 232 pages, by Albert A. Ehrenzweig, Late Professor of Law, University of California, Berkeley, David W. Louisell, Late Professor of Law, University of California, Berkeley and Geoffrey C. Hazard, Jr., Professor of Law, Yale Law School.

Juvenile Courts, 3rd Ed., 1984, 291 pages, by Sanford J. Fox, Professor of Law, Boston College.

Labor Arbitration Law and Practice, 1979, 358 pages, by Dennis R. Nolan, Professor of Law, University of South Carolina.

NUTSHELL SERIES

Labor Law, 1979, 403 pages, by Douglas L. Leslie, Professor of Law, University of Virginia.

Land Use, 1978, 316 pages, by Robert R. Wright, Professor of Law, University of Arkansas, Little Rock and Susan Webber, Professor of Law, University of Arkansas, Little Rock.

Landlord and Tenant Law, 1979, 319 pages, by David S. Hill, Professor of Law, University of Colorado.

Law Study and Law Examinations—Introduction to, 1971, 389 pages, by Stanley V. Kinyon, Late Professor of Law, University of Minnesota.

Legal Interviewing and Counseling, 1976, 353 pages, by Thomas L. Shaffer, Professor of Law, Washington and Lee University.

Legal Research, 4th Ed., 1985, approximately 425 pages, by Morris L. Cohen, Professor of Law and Law Librarian, Yale University.

Legal Writing, 1982, 294 pages, by Dr. Lynn B. Squires and Marjorie Dick Rombauer, Professor of Law, University of Washington.

Legislative Law and Process, 1975, 279 pages, by Jack Davies, Professor of Law, William Mitchell College of Law.

Local Government Law, 2nd Ed., 1983, 404 pages, by David J. McCarthy, Jr., Professor of Law, Georgetown University.

Mass Communications Law, 2nd Ed., 1983, 473 pages, by Harvey L. Zuckman, Professor of Law, Catholic University and Martin J. Gaynes, Lecturer in Law, Temple University.

Medical Malpractice—The Law of, 1977, 340 pages, by Joseph H. King, Professor of Law, University of Tennessee.

Military Law, 1980, 378 pages, by Charles A. Shanor, Professor of Law, Emory University and Timothy P. Terrell, Professor of Law, Emory University.

Oil and Gas, 1983, 443 pages, by John S. Lowe, Professor of Law, University of Tulsa.

Personal Property, 1983, 322 pages, by Barlow Burke, Jr., Professor of Law, American University.

Post-Conviction Remedies, 1978, 360 pages, by Robert Popper, Professor of Law, University of Missouri, Kansas City.

Presidential Power, 1977, 328 pages, by Arthur Selwyn Miller, Professor of Law Emeritus, George Washington University.

Procedure Before Trial, 1972, 258 pages, by Delmar Karlen, Professor of Law Emeritus, New York University.

Products Liability, 2nd Ed., 1981, 341 pages, by Dix W. Noel, Late Professor of Law, University of Tennessee and Jerry J. Phillips, Professor of Law, University of Tennessee.

Professional Responsibility, 1980, 399 pages, by Robert H. Aronson, Professor of Law, University of Washington, and Donald T. Weckstein, Professor of Law, University of San Diego.

Real Estate Finance, 2nd Ed., 1985, approximately 300 pages, by Jon W. Bruce, Professor of Law, Vanderbilt University.

Real Property, 2nd Ed., 1981, 448 pages, by Roger H. Bernhardt, Professor of Law, Golden Gate University.

Regulated Industries, 1982, 394 pages, by Ernest Gellhorn, Dean and Professor of Law, Case Western Reserve University, and Richard J. Pierce, Dean and Professor of Law, University of Pittsburgh.

Remedies, 2nd Ed., 1985, 325 pages, by John F. O'Connell, Professor of Law, Western State University College of Law, Fullerton.

Res Judicata, 1976, 310 pages, by Robert C. Casad, Professor of Law, University of Kansas.

Sales, 2nd Ed., 1981, 370 pages, by John M. Stockton, Professor of Business Law, Wharton School of Finance and Commerce, University of Pennsylvania.

Schools, Students and Teachers—Law of, 1984, 409 pages, by Kern Alexander, Professor of Education, University of Florida and M. David Alexander, Professor, Virginia Tech University.

Sea—Law of, 1984, 264 pages, by Louis B. Sohn, Professor of Law, University of Georgia, and Kristen Gustafson.

Secured Transactions, 2nd Ed., 1981, 391 pages, by Henry J. Bailey, Professor of Law Emeritus, Willamette University.

Securities Regulation, 2nd Ed., 1982, 322 pages, by David L. Ratner, Dean and Professor of Law, University of San Francisco.

Sex Discrimination, 1982, 399 pages, by Claire Sherman Thomas, Lecturer, University of Washington, Women's Studies Department.

Torts—Injuries to Persons and Property, 1977, 434 pages, by Edward J. Kionka, Professor of Law, Southern Illinois University.

Torts—Injuries to Family, Social and Trade Relations, 1979, 358 pages, by Wex S. Malone, Professor of Law Emeritus, Louisiana State University.

Trial Advocacy, 1979, 402 pages, by Paul B. Bergman, Adjunct Professor of Law, University of California, Los Angeles.

Trial and Practice Skills, 1978, 346 pages, by Kenney F. Hegland, Professor of Law, University of Arizona.

Trial, The First—Where Do I Sit? What Do I Say?, 1982, 396 pages, by Steven H. Goldberg, Professor of Law, University of Minnesota.

Unfair Trade Practices, 1982, 444 pages, by Charles R. McManis, Professor of Law, Washington University, St. Louis.

Uniform Commercial Code, 2nd Ed., 1984, 516 pages, by Bradford Stone, Professor of Law, Detroit College of Law.

Uniform Probate Code, 1978, 425 pages, by Lawrence H. Averill, Jr., Dean and Professor of Law, University of Arkansas, Little Rock.

Water Law, 1984, 439 pages, by David H. Getches, Professor of Law, University of Colorado.

Welfare Law—Structure and Entitlement, 1979, 455 pages, by Arthur B. LaFrance, Dean and Professor of Law, Lewis and Clark College, Northwestern School of Law.

Wills and Trusts, 1979, 392 pages, by Robert L. Mennell, Former Professor of Law, Hamline University.

Workers' Compensation and Employee Protection Laws, 1984, 248 pages, by Jack B. Hood, Former Professor of Law, Cumberland School of Law, Samford University and Benjamin A. Hardy, Former Professor of Law, Cumberland School of Law, Samford University.

Hornbook Series

and

Basic Legal Texts

of

WEST PUBLISHING COMPANY

P.O. Box 64526

St. Paul, Minnesota 55164–0526

Administrative Law, Davis' Text on, 3rd Ed., 1972, 617 pages, by Kenneth Culp Davis, Professor of Law, University of San Diego.

Agency and Partnership, Reuschlein & Gregory's Hornbook on the Law of, 1979 with 1981 Pocket Part, 625 pages, by Harold Gill Reuschlein, Professor of Law Emeritus, Villanova University and William A. Gregory, Professor of Law, Georgia State University.

Antitrust, Sullivan's Hornbook on the Law of, 1977, 886 pages, by Lawrence A. Sullivan, Professor of Law, University of California, Berkeley.

Civil Procedure, Friedenthal, Kane and Miller's Hornbook on, Student Ed., 1985, approximately 750 pages, by Jack H. Friedental, Professor of Law, Stanford University, Mary K. Kane, Professor of Law, University of California, Hastings College of the Law and Arthur R. Miller, Professor of Law, Harvard University.

Common Law Pleading, Koffler and Reppy's Hornbook on, 1969, 663 pages, by Joseph H. Koffler, Professor of Law, New York Law School and Alison Reppy, Late Dean and Professor of Law, New York Law School.

Conflict of Laws, Scoles and Hay's Hornbook on, Student Ed., 1982, 1085 pages, by Eugene F. Scoles, Professor of Law,

University of Illinois and Peter Hay, Dean and Professor of Law, University of Illinois.

Constitutional Law, Nowak, Rotunda and Young's Hornbook on, 2nd Ed., Student Ed., 1983, 1172 pages, by John E. Nowak, Professor of Law, University of Illinois, Ronald D. Rotunda, Professor of Law, University of Illinois, and J. Nelson Young, Professor of Law, University of North Carolina.

Contracts, Calamari and Perillo's Hornbook on, 2nd Ed., 1977, 878 pages, by John D. Calamari, Professor of Law, Fordham University and Joseph M. Perillo, Professor of Law, Fordham University.

Contracts, Corbin's One Volume Student Ed., 1952, 1224 pages, by Arthur L. Corbin, Late Professor of Law, Yale University.

Corporate Taxation, Kahn's Handbook on, 3rd Ed., Student Ed., Soft cover, 1981 with 1983 Supplement, 614 pages, by Douglas A. Kahn, Professor of Law, University of Michigan.

Corporations, Henn and Alexander's Hornbook on, 3rd Ed., Student Ed., 1983, 1371 pages, by Harry G. Henn, Professor of Law, Cornell University and John R. Alexander, Member, New York and Hawaii Bars.

Criminal Law, LaFave and Scott's Hornbook on, 1972, 763 pages, by Wayne R. LaFave, Professor of Law, University of Illinois, and Austin Scott, Jr., Late Professor of Law, University of Colorado.

Criminal Procedure, LaFave and Israel's Hornbook on, Student Ed., 1985, approximately 1300 pages, by Wayne R. LaFave, Professor of Law, University of Illinois and Jerold H. Israel, Professor of Law University of Michigan.

Damages, McCormick's Hornbook on, 1935, 811 pages, by Charles T. McCormick, Late Dean and Professor of Law, University of Texas.

Domestic Relations, Clark's Hornbook on, 1968, 754 pages, by Homer H. Clark, Jr., Professor of Law, University of Colorado.

Economics and Federal Antitrust Law, Hovenkamp's Hornbook on, Student Ed., 1985, approximately 375 pages, by Herbert

Hovenkamp, Professor of Law, University of California, Hastings College of the Law.

Environmental Law, Rodgers' Hornbook on, 1977 with 1984 Pocket Part, 956 pages, by William H. Rodgers, Jr., Professor of Law, University of Washington.

Evidence, Lilly's Introduction to, 1978, 486 pages, by Graham C. Lilly, Professor of Law, University of Virginia.

Evidence, McCormick's Hornbook on, 3rd Ed., Student Ed., 1984, 1155 pages, General Editor, Edward W. Cleary, Professor of Law Emeritus, Arizona State University.

Federal Courts, Wright's Hornbook on, 4th Ed., Student Ed., 1983, 870 pages, by Charles Alan Wright, Professor of Law, University of Texas.

Federal Income Taxation of Individuals, Posin's Hornbook on, Student Ed., 1983 with 1985 Pocket Part, 491 pages, by Daniel Q. Posin, Jr., Professor of Law, Southern Methodist University.

Future Interest, Simes' Hornbook on, 2nd Ed., 1966, 355 pages, by Lewis M. Simes, Late Professor of Law, University of Michigan.

Insurance, Keeton's Basic Text on, 1971, 712 pages, by Robert E. Keeton, Professor of Law Emeritus, Harvard University.

Labor Law, Gorman's Basic Text on, 1976, 914 pages, by Robert A. Gorman, Professor of Law, University of Pennsylvania.

Law Problems, Ballentine's, 5th Ed., 1975, 767 pages, General Editor, William E. Burby, Late Professor of Law, University of Southern California.

Legal Writing Style, Weihofen's, 2nd Ed., 1980, 332 pages, by Henry Weihofen, Professor of Law Emeritus, University of New Mexico.

Local Government Law, Reynolds' Hornbook on, 1982, 860 pages, by Osborne M. Reynolds, Professor of Law, University of Oklahoma.

New York Practice, Siegel's Hornbook on, 1978, with 1981–82 Pocket Part, 1011 pages, by David D. Siegel, Professor of Law, Albany Law School of Union University.

Oil and Gas, Hemingway's Hornbook on, 2nd Ed., Student Ed., 1983, 543 pages, by Richard W. Hemingway, Professor of Law, University of Oklahoma.

Poor, Law of the, LaFrance, Schroeder, Bennett and Boyd's Hornbook on, 1973, 558 pages, by Arthur B. LaFrance, Dean and Professor of Law, Lewis and Clark College, Northwestern School of Law, Milton R. Schroeder, Professor of Law, Arizona State University, Robert W. Bennett, Professor of Law, Northwestern University and William E. Boyd, Professor of Law, University of Arizona.

Property, Boyer's Survey of, 3rd Ed., 1981, 766 pages, by Ralph E. Boyer, Professor of Law, University of Miami.

Property, Law of, Cunningham, Whitman and Stoebuck's Hornbook on, Student Ed., 1984, 916 pages, by Roger A. Cunningham, Professor of Law, University of Michigan, Dale A. Whitman, Dean and Professor of Law, University of Missouri–Columbia and William B. Stoebuck, Professor of Law, University of Washington.

Real Estate Finance Law, Osborne, Nelson and Whitman's Hornbook on, (successor to Hornbook on Mortgages), 1979, 885 pages, by George E. Osborne, Late Professor of Law, Stanford University, Grant S. Nelson, Professor of Law, University of Missouri, Columbia and Dale A. Whitman, Dean and Professor of Law, University of Missouri, Columbia.

Real Property, Burby's Hornbook on, 3rd Ed., 1965, 490 pages, by William E. Burby, Late Professor of Law, University of Southern California.

Real Property, Moynihan's Introduction to, 1962, 254 pages, by Cornelius J. Moynihan, Professor of Law, Suffolk University.

Remedies, Dobb's Hornbook on, 1973, 1067 pages, by Dan B. Dobbs, Professor of Law, University of Arizona.

Secured Transactions under the U.C.C., Henson's Hornbook on, 2nd Ed., 1979, with 1979 Pocket Part, 504 pages, by Ray D.

Henson, Professor of Law, University of California, Hastings College of the Law.

Securities Regulation, Hazen's Hornbook on the Law of, Student Ed., 1985, approximately 665 pages, by Thomas Lee Hazen, Professor of Law, University of North Carolina.

Torts, Prosser and Keeton's Hornbook on, 5th Ed., Student Ed., 1984, 1286 pages, by William L. Prosser, Late Dean and Professor of Law, University of California, Berkeley, Page Keeton, Professor of Law Emeritus, University of Texas, Dan B. Dobbs, Professor of Law, University of Arizona, Robert E. Keeton, Professor of Law Emeritus, Harvard University and David G. Owen, Professor of Law, University of South Carolina.

Trial Advocacy, Jeans' Handbook on, Student Ed., Soft cover, 1975, by James W. Jeans, Professor of Law, University of Missouri, Kansas City.

Trusts, Bogert's Hornbook on, 5th Ed., 1973, 726 pages, by George G. Bogert, Late Professor of Law, University of Chicago and George T. Bogert, Attorney, Chicago, Illinois.

Urban Planning and Land Development Control, Hagman's Hornbook on, 1971, 706 pages, by Donald G. Hagman, Late Professor of Law, University of California, Los Angeles.

Uniform Commercial Code, White and Summers' Hornbook on, 2nd Ed., 1980, 1250 pages, by James J. White, Professor of Law, University of Michigan and Robert S. Summers, Professor of Law, Cornell University.

Wills, Atkinson's Hornbook on, 2nd Ed., 1953, 975 pages, by Thomas E. Atkinson, Late Professor of Law, New York University.

Advisory Board

REAL ESTATE FINANCE

IN A

NUTSHELL

SECOND EDITION

By

JON W. BRUCE

Professor of Law
Vanderbilt University

ST. PAUL, MINN.
WEST PUBLISHING CO.
1985

COPYRIGHT © 1979 By WEST PUBLISHING CO.
COPYRIGHT © 1985 By WEST PUBLISHING CO.
                50 West Kellogg Boulevard
                P.O. Box 64526
                St. Paul, Minnesota 55164–0526

Printed in the United States of America

Library of Congress Cataloging in Publication Data

Bruce, Jon W., 1944–
  Real estate finance in a nutshell.

  (Nutshell series)
  1. Mortgages—United States. I. Title. II. Series.
KF695.Z9B78 1985   346.7304'364   84–26919
ISBN 0–314–85866–0   347.3064364

    Bruce Real Est. Fin.2nd Ed. NS

To my wife
Barbara Edmonson Bruce

*

PREFACE

This book is a concise textual treatment of the law of real estate finance. It is designed primarily to help law students negotiate a law school course on the subject. Hopefully it will also serve other members of the legal community as a general reference work and starting point for research. In this regard, a table of secondary authorities is included at the end of the book to assist the reader who desires to make further inquiry into an area introduced in the text.

The material in this Nutshell is organized into detailed outline form for two reasons. First, the format is designed to give students a thorough overview of the subject and a set of pegs upon which to hang information gleaned from classroom discussion. Second, the relative rigidity of this style helped me resist the urge to write a law review type work complete with mountains of footnotes. Such an approach is, of course, inconsistent with the purpose of this Nutshell Series. Exhaustive discussion, therefore, has been sacrificed in favor of summarization and clarity. The reader is requested to keep this in mind as he or she proceeds through these materials.

One final word about the book. Real estate finance is like most property law, overgrown with rules. The rules, of course, are stated here, but so are the underlying theories. This is designed to give the student a better understanding of the rules and an opportunity to begin critically examining them.

I wish to say thanks to the following people: my wife Barb for her patience and understanding during the preparation of both editions of this book; John Stark and Dan Sterner of the Indianapolis bar for giving me an excellent introduction to the practice of real estate finance law; Doug Mulligan my research assistant on the first edition for his tireless research efforts; and Jim Gillespie for his encouragement and helpful comments.

JON W. BRUCE

OUTLINE

**CHAPTER 3. REAL ESTATE FINANCING
DEVICES**

CHAPTER 4. THE UNDERLYING OBLIGATION

OUTLINE

OUTLINE

XXVII

CHAPTER 5. THE MORTGAGED PROPERTY

CHAPTER 6. TRANSFER OF THE MORTGAGOR'S INTEREST

OUTLINE

OUTLINE

CHAPTER 7. TRANSFER OF THE MORTGAGEE'S INTEREST

OUTLINE

OUTLINE

CHAPTER 9. PRIORITIES

Page

III. Selected Priority Problems—Continued

CHAPTER 10. FORECLOSURE

OUTLINE

CHAPTER 11. FINANCING COOPERATIVES AND CONDOMINIUMS

OUTLINE

CHAPTER 12. REFORM

OUTLINE

APPENDICES

*

REAL ESTATE FINANCE
IN A
NUTSHELL

*

CHAPTER 1

INTRODUCTION TO THE LAW OF REAL ESTATE FINANCE

This introductory chapter presents an overview of the law of real estate finance. Because the mortgage is the cornerstone of real estate finance, it is the focal point of this chapter and for that matter the entire book.

I. THE MORTGAGE CONCEPT

A. Definition and Description

A mortgage is the transfer of an interest in land as security for the performance of an obligation. The typical mortgage transaction is relatively uncomplicated. A landowner borrows money from an institutional lender and enters a written agreement with the lender that the landowner's real estate is collateral for repayment of the loan. In legal terminology the landowner-borrower is a mortgagor, the lender is a mortgagee, and the agreement is a mortgage. If the mortgagor fails to pay the mortgage loan, the mortgagee may enforce his security interest by using appropriate foreclosure procedures to have the mortgaged land sold to satisfy the debt. *See* Appendices A, B, and C for sample mortgage forms. (In all of the illustrations in this book

[1]

"MR" refers to the mortgagor and "ME" refers to the mortgagee).

B. The Obligation/Security Distinction

A mortgage exists solely as security for an underlying obligation, usually a promissory note. Consequently, it lives, travels, and dies with the obligation.

Illustration: MR executes a note and mortgage to ME. ME assigns the note to A, but through inadvertence fails to assign the mortgage. Nonetheless, the mortgage follows the note into A's hands by operation of law.

Illustration: MR executes a note and mortgage to ME. MR pays ME in full. ME returns the note to MR, but does not release the mortgage. ME has no further rights under the mortgage. The security interest created by the mortgage lapses when the underlying debt is satisfied.

C. Statute of Frauds

A mortgage involves the transfer of an interest in land. Thus, it must be in writing to comply with the Statute of Frauds. Equitable principles, however, may dictate that a mortgage arises by operation of law or is enforceable even though unwritten.

Illustration: MR asks ME for a loan to pay several bills. ME makes the loan upon MR's oral promise that his farm is security for the loan. MR defaults. ME seeks to foreclose and have the farm sold. ME has no right to do so, because the oral promise is unenforceable. As a general rule, the mere lending of money does not constitute sufficient part performance to take the transaction out of the Statute of Frauds.

Illustration: MR asks ME for a loan to purchase a specific parcel of real estate. ME makes the loan upon MR's oral promise to give ME a mortgage on the property to be purchased. MR uses the loan proceeds to purchase the property, but refuses to execute a mortgage to ME as promised. MR defaults. ME seeks to foreclose and have the land sold. ME generally may do so, because the oral promise to give the mortgage is enforceable under either of two theories: (1) An equitable mortgage arises by operation of law in order to permit ME to obtain payment out of the product of his loan. It, therefore, is not subject to the Statute of Frauds. (2) Hardship on ME plus the use of the loan proceeds to purchase the property constitutes sufficient part performance to satisfy the policy of the Statute of Frauds.

II. HISTORICAL DEVELOPMENT OF THE MORTGAGE

Real estate finance is best understood by one who is thoroughly acquainted with the development of the mortgage concept. An abbreviated jaunt through legal history, therefore, is in order. During this excursion, note how the legal pendulum swings first in favor of the mortgagee, then in favor of the mortgagor and so on, back and forth, throughout history.

A. The Defeasible Fee as a Financing Device

At early English common law, a mortgage was simply a deed of a defeasible fee from the mortgagor to the mortgagee. If the debt was repaid at maturity, or "law day" in common law parlance, the mortgagee's estate terminated and the mortgagor again owned the land. If, however, the debt was not paid at maturity, the mortgagee's defeasible fee became a fee simple absolute. Because the law courts strictly enforced the time for payment, the mortgagor lost his land even if he tendered payment one day late.

B. Equity of Redemption

1. *Creation and Growth*

In order to mitigate the harsh results of this common law approach, the equity courts intervened. If a mortgagor could establish a sound reason for failing to perform as agreed in the mortgage, equity would permit him to recover his land by paying the debt after the maturity date. This right of late payment eventually was extended to all mortgagors without regard to the existence of individual equities and became known as the equity of redemption. *See* Ch. 8, pp. 152–155.

2. *Preservation/Clogging*

Equity courts have always zealously preserved the mortgagor's equity of redemption. Any clause in the mortgage or in a contemporaneous agreement that has the effect of eliminating or

[4]

impairing the mortgagor's right to redeem is termed clogging and is prohibited. Otherwise a mortgage could be transformed into a defeasible fee by the use of a simple waiver clause. The courts' protective approach in this regard gave rise to the maxim: "once a mortgage, always a mortgage."

Illustration: MR executes a mortgage to ME. At the same time he gives ME an option to purchase the mortgaged land for a nominal sum if he defaults. The option is unenforceable as a contemporaneous clog on the mortgagor's equity of redemption. It is really a disguised waiver. *See* Ch. 6, pp. 103–104 for a discussion of when the mortgagee may properly acquire the mortgaged property.

C. Foreclosure

1. *Strict Foreclosure*

The creation of an immutable equity of redemption placed the mortgagee in a difficult position. The defaulting mortgagor's right to redeem effectively prevented the mortgagee from selling or improving the mortgaged property. The English equity courts thus came to the aid of mortgagees by developing the concept of foreclosure of the equity of redemption. After default and at the mortgagee's request, the equity courts set a time period within which the mortgagor was required to pay the debt or forever lose the right to redeem. If the mortgagor failed to pay within the period specified, the mortgagee obtained a fee simple absolute. This method of terminating the mortgagor's equity of redemption became known as strict foreclosure.

2. *Foreclosure by Sale*

Strict foreclosure was inherently unfair to the mortgagor because the value of the mortgaged land acquired by the mortgagee frequently exceeded the amount of the debt. The legal pendulum, consequently, began to swing back in favor of mortgagors. This time our state courts played an active role. (The rest of this chapter deals exclusively with the evolution of real estate finance law in this country). Equity again readjusted the conflicting interests of the parties by requiring foreclosure of the mortgagor's equity of redemption via public sale. The proceeds of the sale were applied first to expenses, then to pay the mortgage debt. Any surplus was given the mortgagor. If the proceeds were insufficient to satisfy the mortgage debt, the mortgagee could obtain a deficiency judgment against the mortgagor. This foreclosure by sale procedure is the primary method of foreclosure in the United States today. Strict foreclosure is available in only limited circumstances. *See* Ch. 10, p. 193.

Two variations on the foreclosure by sale theme exist: foreclosure by judicial sale and foreclosure by power of sale. Foreclosure by judicial sale involves a court supervised procedure that is often expensive and time consuming. Nonetheless, because judicial supervision protects the mortgagor, foreclosure by judicial sale is available in all states and is the exclusive method of foreclosure in many jurisdictions. *See* Ch. 10, pp. 180–188.

Power of sale foreclosure derives its name from the fact that in some jurisdictions the mortgage may include a provision granting the mortgagee the power to sell the mortgaged property without court supervision. This type of foreclosure is also sometimes called foreclosure by advertisement because of the manner by which the mortgagee typically gives notice of the sale. *See* Ch. 10, pp. 188–193.

D. Statutory Redemption

Statutes in several jurisdictions give the mortgagor an opportunity to redeem his property even after his equity of redemption has been foreclosed. This right, referred to as statutory redemption, exists in about one-half of the states. Generally the mortgagor is given a set period of time after the foreclosure sale, often one year, to pay the foreclosure sale price and redeem the land. *See* Ch. 10, pp. 194–197.

III. MORTGAGE THEORIES

Although it is generally recognized that a mortgage is a transfer of a security interest in land, controversy exists regarding the precise nature of the mortgagee's interest. During the evolu-

tion of the mortgage from a defeasible conveyance to a security device, the courts did not
adequately deal with the interrelated problem of
possession. Today the states handle this unresolved possession problem in three different
ways.

A. Title Theory

Some states referred to as title theory jurisdictions continue to follow the original common law
view that a mortgage conveys legal title to the
mortgagee. In these jurisdictions the mortgagee
receives the right to possession of the mortgage
property when the mortgage is executed on the
theory that possession follows legal title. Most
title theory states lie in the eastern part of the
country where early common law had the greatest impact.

B. Intermediate Theory

A few eastern states still recognize the mortgage as a conveyance of a defeasible fee in form,
but limit the mortgagee's right to possession in a
manner consistent with the view that the mortgage creates simply a security interest. These
states, called intermediate theory jurisdictions,
give the mortgagor the right to possession until
default and the mortgagee the right thereafter.

C. Lien Theory

In the majority of states the mortgage is
viewed as giving the mortgagee a lien on the

[8]

mortgaged property, not legal title. Thus, in these lien theory jurisdictions the mortgagor retains the right to possession until foreclosure.

D. The Practical Significance of Mortgage Theories

It is important to note that even in title and intermediate theory states, the mortgagee's rights as legal title-holder generally have been eliminated where unnecessary to protect his security interest. The primary difference among the title, intermediate and lien theories, therefore, is with respect to the mortgagee's right to possession. *See* Ch. 8, pp. 142–143.

IV. MODERN FINANCING FORMATS

Although the mortgage is still the foundation of real estate finance, many sophisticated financing variations exist today. The complex financing formats that have evolved over the past several years often involve the use of a combination of mortgages, leases, installment land contracts, or outright conveyances. In subsequent chapters, you will become well acquainted with fundamental mortgage law and will be introduced to a wide variety of other real estate financing devices.

CHAPTER 2

THE MORTGAGE MARKET

The principles of real estate finance law discussed in this book are meaningful only when considered in light of the practical aspects of mortgage lending. This chapter, therefore, deals with the structure and operation of the mortgage market.

I. THE PURPOSE OF FINANCING

A. General

The purpose of the mortgage loan is the initial point of inquiry. Distinctions in two categories are important: (1) is the mortgage loan money to be used for construction or permanent financing? and (2) is the mortgage loan to be secured by residential or commercial property? The answers to these questions determine to a large extent the source of the loan and the terms of the mortgage agreement.

B. Construction/Permanent Financing

1. Description and Distinction

A construction mortgage loan, sometimes referred to as an interim loan, is a short-term loan to an owner-developer for the construction of improvements on the real estate that secures the loan.

Illustration: MR is a real estate developer who wishes to build an apartment building on land he already owns. ME loans MR money to construct the project, to be disbursed as construction progresses. The loan is secured by a mortgage on the land and improvements and is due in 18 months. ME collects only interest during the 18 months. This is a simplified construction mortgage loan.

A permanent mortgage loan, sometimes referred to as a final loan, is a long-term loan to the owner of the real estate that secures the loan.

Illustration: MR obtains a loan from ME to purchase a house and gives ME a mortgage on the house as security. The loan is for a 30 year term and is payable in equal monthly installments of principal and interest. This is a typical residential permanent mortgage loan.

2. The Relationship Between Construction and Permanent Lenders

Construction and permanent mortgage loans often work hand-in-hand; upon completion of construction the construction lender is usually paid by funds obtained from a permanent lender. The construction lender then either assigns his mortgage to the permanent lender or releases the construction loan mortgage so that the permanent lender's mortgage has first lien priority. This, of course, has all been arranged ahead of time by the parties involved. The borrower first obtains a loan commitment from the permanent lender, then secures construction financing. The arrangement between the borrower and the construction lender is set out in a construction loan agreement. Before construction funds are advanced, the lenders enter a "buy-sell" agreement whereby the permanent lender agrees to "takeout" the construction lender upon completion of construction.

3.   The Construction Lender's Special Risks

a.   Nature of the Risk and Minimizing It

A construction mortgage loan involves a greater risk than a permanent mortgage loan. The construction lender's investment is fully secured only when the project is completed in accordance with the plans and specifications upon which the parties originally agreed. Thus, the construction lender must closely supervise construction and advance funds under the construction loan agreement as the project properly progresses. *See* Ch. 4, pp. 69–70. As compensation for assuming this burden, he charges a higher rate of interest than does the permanent lender.

The construction lender also attempts to minimize his risk of loss in the event the project should encounter construction difficulty. First, he takes steps to insure that his mortgage has first lien priority. *See* Ch. 4, pp. 64–69; Ch. 9, pp. 158–159. Second, he may require the mortgagor to personally guaranty completion of construction. Third, often in lieu of the second alternative, he may require the mortgagor to obtain performance and payment bonds in their joint names. The dual obligee performance bond assures the lender that the project will be completed in accordance with the construction contract. The dual obligee payment bond assures him that all charges for labor or material used in construction will be paid. This prevents loss resulting from the attachment of any mechanics' liens that might gain priority over the construction loan mortgage, but at the same time raises the possibility that the bonding company may seek to be subrogated to the rights of mechanics' lienors. Hence, as a practical matter, the payment bond may afford the lender no protection at all. *See* Ch. 9, pp. 169–172.

b. Liability for Construction Defects — *very rare for constr. lender*

Recently construction lenders have faced an unexpected additional risk, liability for faulty construction. A few courts have held that a construction lender is liable for construction defects if he goes beyond the domain of the usual construction lender and becomes an active participant in the construction enterprise. The Supreme Court of California was the first court to adopt this approach. Connor v. Great Western Savings and Loan Association, 69 Cal.2d 850, 73

[*13*]

Cal.Rptr. 369, 447 P.2d 609 (1968). But almost immediately after the court's decision, the California legislature enacted a statute purporting to limit construction lenders' liability for construction defects. Cal.Civ.Code § 3434 (West 1970). Although the doctrine fashioned by the California court in *Connor* has been recognized elsewhere, it has rarely if ever been employed outside California to impose liability on a particular construction lender.

C. Residential/Commercial Property

The distinction between residential and commercial mortgage loans is important because some lenders specialize in making loans secured by a particular kind of property. Residential mortgage loans are loans secured by any form of residential property; for example, single family dwellings, duplexes, apartments and condominiums. sometimes residential mortgage loans are further broken down into loans on one-to-four family properties called home loans and loans on multi-family units. Commercial mortgage loans are merely loans made on non-residential property; for example, shopping centers, hotels, office buildings, warehouses and manufacturing plants.

II. ORIGINATING/SERVICING/HOLDING

In order to fully understand the mortgage market, one must appreciate the differences among originating, servicing and holding mortgage loans. The institution that initially advances funds "originates" the mortgage loan. The organization that collects the mortgage payment from and otherwise deals directly with the borrower "services" the loan. The lender that owns the mortgage loan at any one time "holds" the loan. Many times the same entity originates, holds and services the loan. Almost as often, the originator sells the mortgage loan to a new holder who has someone, frequently the originator, service the loan for him.

III. SOURCES OF REAL ESTATE FINANCING

The institutions that make mortgage loan funds available form the foundation of the mortgage market. The most significant sources of real estate financing are described in general terms in this section.

A. Commercial Banks

Commercial banks are depository institutions chartered by either a state or the federal government. They make only a limited number of permanent mortgage loans because they must maintain liquidity to meet demand deposits. Construction lending is usually a more significant part of their mortgage loan operation, the yields are higher and the bank's funds are not tied up for prolonged periods.

B. Savings and Loan Associations

Savings and loan associations are also either state or federally chartered. They are restricted as to the type of mortgage investments they may make, but less so now than a decade ago. Savings and loan associations are specialists in housing finance and heavily invest in both construction and permanent residential mortgages. In 1982, they originated about one-third of all residential mortgages in the country.

C. Mutual Savings Banks

Mutual savings banks are state chartered institutions located primarily in the northeast. They operate in the same general sphere as savings and loan associations, but tend to concentrate their mortgage investments in permanent residential mortgages acquired from other institutional lenders.

D. Life Insurance Companies

Life insurance companies are state chartered and subject to local insurance law. Because of a relatively predictable flow of funds, life insurance companies are heavily involved in permanent financing of both commercial and multi-unit residential projects.

The long term nature of their mortgage investments, however, puts life insurance companies in a difficult position during periods of rapid inflation. As a consequence, they frequently require the right to participate in income from the project being financed. *See* Ch. 4, pp. 76–77.

E. Pension Funds

Public and private employee pension funds are an increasing source of capital for real estate financing, particularly in the area of permanent commercial mortgages and mortgage-backed securities.

F. Real Estate Investment Trusts

Real estate investment trusts ("REITs") are a product of federal tax legislation of the early 1960's designed to give the small investor an opportunity to participate in sophisticated and diverse real estate investments. A REIT is usually formed as a business trust in which investors purchase beneficial interests called shares. If the REIT meets a number of tax requirements, it will not be taxed on income and capital gains distributed to the shareholders.

The first qualified REITs were "equity" trusts that developed or purchased income producing commercial property. They were not generally successful. In the late 1960's, however, REITs that engaged solely in mortgage lending, became popular. Although mortgage REITs made permanent loans, they became important primarily as suppliers of construction financing. Consequently, the building slump of the middle 1970's hit mortgage REITs hard. Some went bankrupt and many others barely survived. Although some equity REITs made a comeback in the early 1980's, the future role of REITs in real estate finance is uncertain.

G. Mortgage Banking Companies

Mortgage banking companies are corporations organized under state law. Although mortgage bankers are a source of some real estate financing funds, they are more important as intermediaries between borrowers and other lenders.

There are two major ways in which mortgage bankers perform their intermediary function. (1) They originate home mortgage loans for sale to institutional investors and then service the loan for the investor who holds it. (2) They put commercial borrowers, construction lenders and permanent lenders in contact with one another.

In performing the latter service, mortgage bankers often facilitate the operation of the overall transaction by financing projects for a short time between the completion of construction and the sale to the permanent investor. They frequently obtain funds for this interim financing from a commercial bank under a line of credit secured by an assignment of the mortgage loan involved. This arrangement is known as mortgage warehousing. Mortgage bankers also utilize this financing technique to enable them to serve as construction lenders in their own right.

In either case the mortgage banker realizes a profit from mortgage warehousing by borrowing money, often at the commercial bank's prime interest rate, and then lending it to the developer at a higher rate of return.

H. Other Sources

Credit unions, individuals, syndications, service corporations, state development agencies, and community housing authorities are other less significant sources of real estate investment capital.

1. *Credit Unions*

Federal credit unions were recently authorized to offer residential mortgage loans. Their impact on the mortgage market has been slight thus far.

2. *Individuals*

Individual sellers sometimes take back a purchase money mortgage on the property being sold. These transactions, however, constitute only a small percentage of the total mortgage loans outstanding at any one time.

3. *Syndications*

Syndications are groups of individual real estate investors often formed as limited partnerships. Most syndications, however, invest by purchasing realty rather than by making mortgage loans.

4. *Service Corporations*

Service corporations are organized by savings and loan associations within the state in which they operate. Their funds may be invested in real estate in a wide variety of ways.

5. *State Development Agencies*

State development agencies have been created by many state legislatures to deal with intrastate housing problems by financing the construction of low and modern income housing. The development agencies generally have the power to raise funds by issuing tax exempt bonds.

6. *Community Housing Authorities*

Many cities have established a housing authority that finances the construction of low and modern income housing from the sale of tax exempt bonds.

IV. OBTAINING REAL ESTATE FINANCING

A. Application and Commitment

Once a potential source of funds is identified, the borrower secures the mortgage loan through the process of application and commitment. The borrower initiates the process by making a formal or informal mortgage loan application to the lender who evaluates it in light of the risk involved.

The risk in mortgage financing is a two-tier one. First, the lender must assess the borrower's financial position with a view to predicting the likelihood that he will pay the underlying obligation. Second, the lender must anticipate default and decide whether the mortgaged property will produce a sufficient amount at a foreclosure sale to pay the mortgage debt.

If the lender determines that the overall risk is acceptable, he will issue a loan commitment detailing the amount, term, interest rate, and other pertinent items. The length, formality, and specificity of the commitment varies from lender to lender and loan to loan. Commercial loan commitments naturally are rather complex and usually include a provision for a nonrefundable commitment fee. When the borrower accepts the commitment, a binding contract for a mortgage loan is created.

B. The Mortgage Loan Contract

Mortgage loan contracts are a frequent source of litigation. Two areas are particularly controversial: nonrefundable commitment fees and the borrower's remedy for breach.

1. *Nonrefundable Commitment Fees*

The commitment fee issue arises when a borrower decides not to go through with the loan and then demands return of the "nonrefundable" commitment fee on the ground the lender has done nothing to earn it. The courts have consistently rejected this contention and held that the lender is entitled to the commitment fee either as liquidated damages for breach of contract or as compensation for holding the money available for loan to the borrower.

2. Borrower's Remedy for Lender's Breach

On the other hand, when the lender refuses to complete the loan in accordance with the commitment, questions arise regarding the borrower's remedy for breach of contract. Although the transfer of a security interest in real property is an aspect of the contemplated loan, the borrower generally is not entitled to specific performance. Damages at law are normally considered adequate to compensate him for any loss he may have suffered by reason of the lender's failure to advance the promised funds. Some authorities, however, argue that the borrower should be entitled to specific performance of the mortgage loan contract when money market conditions prevent him from obtaining a similar loan elsewhere.

Case

V. LOAN PARTICIPATIONS (INCLUDING MORTGAGE–BACKED SECURITIES)

A lender is sometimes presented with the opportunity to make an attractive loan, but does not have the entire loan amount conveniently available. Instead of losing the loan, the lender may ask other lenders to provide a share of the funds.

An arrangement of this kind is known as a loan participation. The originating mortgagee is the "lead" lender and the others are participants. The participants' interests in the loan are usually evidenced by participation certificates issued by the lead lender who holds the loan documents, collects payments and disburses the appropriate share to each investor. *See* Ch. 7, p. 126.

A special type of participation involves the sale of an undivided interest in a large pool of mortgage loans. The Government National Mortgage Association, the Federal National Mortgage Association, and the Federal Home Loan Mortgage Corporation utilize such mortgage-backed securities to stimulate private investment in housing. The Government National Mortgage Association's "pass-through" program is an early and well-known example of this type of participation. In that program the periodic mortgage payments made by mortgagors in the pool are distributed among the investors (participants) in proportion to their investments. The Government National Mortgage Association guarantees that the investors will be paid even if mortgagors in the pool fail to make their mortgage payments.

Following the success of public mortgage-backed securities, private sponsors entered the marketplace with similar offerings. Both forms of "participation" have achieved a substantial position in the mortgage market.

VI. SECONDARY FINANCING

Several lenders may independently acquire security interests in the same property by utilizing the mortage market technique known as secondary financing.

A. The Basics

1. *The Creation of Junior Mortgages*

Because the modern mortgage is a security interest in land, a mortgagor is free to mortgage his property to as many lenders as are willing to make loans to him. The placing of a second, third or even fourth mortgage on land is termed secondary financing. The second and subsequent mortgages are categorized as junior mortgages.

Illustration: MR executes a mortgage to ME–1. MR then executes a second mortgage to ME–2 and finally a third mortgage to ME–3. All mortgages are valid. MR gave ME–1 only a security interest in the land, not ownership. The second and third mortgages held by ME–2 and ME–3 are referred to as junior mortgages.

Illustration: O owns a house subject to a $40,000 mortgage held by B bank. O desires to sell the house for $50,000. P agrees to purchase it at that price, but has no ready cash and is unable to obtain a first mortgage loan for the full amount of the purchase price. The parties, therefore, agree to the following arrangement in order to insure that the sale is consummated. O conveys the house to P subject to the existing $40,000 mortgage that P assumes and agrees to pay. *See* Ch. 6, pp. 98–103.

P gives O a $10,000 note for the balance of the purchase price and a second mortgage on the house as security for its payment. B bank's $40,000 first mortgage and O's $10,000 second mortgage are both valid liens on the property.

2. *The Importance of the Mortgagor's "Equity"*

Lenders make junior mortgage loans only if the market value of the mortgaged property exceeds the unpaid balance of a prior mortgage. The difference is known as the mortgagor's equity. The use of the term "equity" in this context is really a convenient way of stating the value of the mortgagor's equity of redemption.

A mortgagor's equity may accumulate in two ways: (1) the principal balance due on the existing mortgage loan may be reduced by partial payment and (2) the mortgaged property may appreciate in value.

Illustration: MR owns a ranch worth $100,000. MR obtains a $100,000 loan from ME–1 secured by a mortgage on the ranch. (Rarely will a mortgagor be able to obtain 100% financing, but it is assumed to be available here for purposes of illustration). MR has $0 equity in the ranch, but still has an equity of redemption. Five years later the ranch has appreciated to a market value of $110,000 and MR has paid the principal on the note down to $90,000. MR, therefore, has $20,000 equity in the ranch. MR needs cash, so he obtains a $15,000 loan from ME–2 secured by a second mortgage on the ranch. After this transaction MR has $5,000 equity.

3. The Risk and the Rate

Junior mortgage loans involve a relatively high risk because the secondary lender's security interest extends only to the value of the land in excess of prior liens. Hence, lenders generally make junior mortgage loans for a shorter term and at a higher interest rate than first mortgage loans.

> *Illustration*: Assume the same facts as in the immediately preceding illustration except that MR fails to pay the loans to ME–1 and ME–2. Both mortgagees foreclose and sale of the ranch produces $100,000 after expenses. ME–1 receives $90,000, the unpaid balance on the first mortgage loan. ME–2 receives $10,000. In reality, ME–2's $15,000 second mortgage loan was only partially secured.

B. Beyond the Basics/Wraparound Mortgages

The wraparound mortgage is a recent innovation in secondary financing. This increasingly popular financing device can be used either to derive additional funds from mortgaged real estate or to finance the purchase of such property. In either case, the wraparound mortgage is like a typical second mortgage in that it attaches to realty already encumbered by a mortgage. Its unique feature is that the face amount of the wraparound mortgage is equal to the amount actually disbursed to the mortgagor plus the unpaid balance of the prior encumbrance. The mortgagor's payments on the wraparound mortgage, therefore, cover both the money advanced

[*26*]

under the wraparound mortgage and the amounts due on the first mortgage. The wraparound mortgagee simply takes a portion of the payment he receives and makes the necessary payment on the original mortgage.

The interest rate on the face amount of the wraparound mortgage is generally higher than the rate on the first mortgage, but slightly below the current market interest rate. The result is that the wraparound mortgagee receives a higher than current interest rate on the money actually advanced. This is because he collects an interest differential on the first mortgage payments as they pass through his hands in addition to interest on the funds he disbursed. At the same time, the wraparound mortgagor pays less interest than he would have if he had obtained the face amount of the wraparound loan at current rates and paid off the existing first mortgage.

Illustration: Several years ago MR mortgaged his office building to ME–1 as security for a $1,000,000 loan at 9% interest per annum. The mortgage loan has been paid down to $700,000 and MR desires to get his $300,000 "equity" out of the project. (In this illustration it is assumed that the office building has had a constant value of $1,000,000 and that 100% financing is available). MR could refinance by borrowing $1,000,000 at the current interest rate of 12%, paying off the first mortgage and using the $300,000 as he desires. As an alternative, MR could obtain a conventional second mortgage loan of $300,000 at the current interest rate of 15%. MR, however, would like to avoid the significant increase in interest rate that would occur by use of either alternative. He, therefore, obtains a wraparound mortgage loan from W–ME in the amount of $1,000,000 at 11% interest. W–ME disburses only $300,000 to MR, but receives payments from MR covering both the $300,000 advanced and the unpaid balance of the first mortgage, all at 11% interest. W–ME passes the payments on the first mortgage to ME–1 after removing the interest differential (2%). W–ME thereby receives 11% interest on the $300,000 he advanced and 2% on the $700,000 balance on the first loan, an overall interest rate well in excess of the stated rate of 11%. At the same time MR pays only 11% on the $1,000,000, 1% below the current interest rate on first mortgage loans.

Illustration: O owns a farm subject to a first mortgage in favor of ME–1. MR purchases the farm from O. MR assumes the first mortgage and executes a wraparound mortgage to O in the amount of the purchase price less the down payment. This transaction is a purchase money wraparound mortgage. It is structured and administered the same as the wraparound mortgage described in the immediately preceding illustration.

VII. FEDERAL GOVERNMENT INVOLVEMENT IN THE FINANCING PROCESS

In the last fifty years Congress has made numerous attempts to improve housing conditions in this country. Its legislative activity has had a considerable impact on the mortgage market.

This section discusses the federal government's involvement in the financing process via housing subsidies, mortgage insurance, secondary mortgage market support institutions, and miscellaneous other means.

A. Housing Subsidies

Some Congressional action in the real estate finance area is designed to produce more and better housing for low and moderate income families through housing subsidies administered by the Department of Housing and Urban Development ("HUD"). The form of the subsidy varies greatly from program to program.

B. Mortgage Insurance and Guaranty Program

A less direct but equally significant form of government involvement in the real estate financing process is the federal mortgage insurance and guaranty program administered by the Federal Housing Administration ("FHA") and the Veterans Administration ("VA"). The program encourages private institutional lenders to make residential mortgage loans to borrowers who otherwise might not qualify. This is accomplished by insuring or guarantying mortgagees against loss on certain residential loans. In essence, the insurance or guaranty takes the place of a large down-payment.

For many years, FHA and VA were required to set a periodically adjusted maximum insurable interest rate for qualifying loans. Because this interest rate was consistently below the current conventional mortgage loan interest rate, lenders assessed a charge for making an FHA or VA mortgage loan. The charge, expressed in terms of discount points, varied depending upon the difference at the time between the conventional loan interest rate and the FHA and VA maximum insurable interest rate. (One discount point equals one percent of the loan amount.)

In late 1983, however, Congress eliminated the maximum insurable interest rate system for FHA mortgages thereby allowing the interest rate for such loans to fluctuate with changes in the mortgage money market as does the interest rate for conventional loans. Pub.L. No. 98–181, § 404 (1983). VA mortgages remain subject to a set ceiling.

Illustration: MR contracts to purchase O's house. MR obtains a VA purchase money mortgage loan from ME in the amount of $30,000 payable over a 30 year term at the current maximum insurable interest rate of 13% per annum. The current interest rate on a similar conventional loan is 13½% per annum. ME, therefore, charges 4 points ($1,200) as compensation for making the loan at a less than competitive interest rate. (One point will increase the effective interest yield approximately ⅛% over the full term of the loan.) Because regulations do not permit the borrower to pay these points, the seller usually does so, but only after negotiating the sale price with this obligation in mind.

Although FHA and VA mortgages are similar, they differ in at least three important ways. First, FHA mortgage loans may be obtained by members of the general public. VA mortgage loans are available only to veterans. Second, FHA insures eligible mortgage loans. VA generally issues a guaranty of partial repayment. VA borrowers, therefore, do not pay annual mortgage insurance premiums as do FHA borrowers. Third, FHA regulations require the borrower to make a small down payment. VA regulations do not require one.

Private companies have also entered the field of mortgage insurance. These private mortgage insurers cover the top 20% or 25% of a mortgagee's loss. They are gaining in popularity largely by reason of their ability to process mortgage loans in a more efficient manner than either FHA or VA.

The growth of private mortgage insurance has made ninety and ninety-five percent conventional home mortgage loans available. For many years institutional lenders were prohibited by regulation from making such high loan-to-value loans. Lending institutions, however, are now generally authorized to make up to ninety or ninety-five percent loans if appropriate private mortgage insurance is obtained to cover the increased risk.

C. Secondary Mortgage Market Support Institutions

Congress also has created several institutions designed to maintain a national secondary market for residential mortgages. The policy underlying this secondary mortgage market approach is that the support institutions can promote the even distribution of real estate investment capital throughout the country by buying mortgages from originators and selling them to investors. (Distinguish the secondary mortgage market which involves the sale of first mortgages from secondary financing which involves the placing of junior mortgages on already encumbered land).

The institutions charged with responsibility for maintaining a viable secondary mortgage market are the Federal National Mortgage Association ("FNMA" or "Fannie Mae"), the Government National Mortgage Association ("GNMA" or "Ginnie Mae") and the Federal Home Loan Mortgage Corporation ("FHLMC" or "Freddie Mac.") Each organization plays a slightly different role in this loosely constructed system.

FNMA is the oldest and most important element of the secondary mortgage market. Originally part of FHA, it is now privately owned, but subject to considerable governmental control. FNMA buys and sells FHA and VA mortgages in order to improve the nationwide distribution of investment capital available for residential mortgage financing. It also deals in conventional mortgages to a lesser extent. Recently FNMA has been active in issuing mortgage-backed securities.

GNMA, a 1968 spinoff from FNMA, is a government owned entity within the Department of Housing and Urban Development. GNMA performs a variety of special assistance, management, and liquidation functions. It also is involved in the secondary mortgage market via special mortgage investment programs such as the "pass-through" mortgage-backed securities program discussed earlier in this chapter.

FHLMC is a privately owned corporation with membership in the Federal Home Loan Bank System. It was created in 1970 to establish a secondary mortgage market for conventional mortgages originated by federal savings and loan associations. It performs this function in good part by assembling pools of conventional mortgages and selling securities backed by these pooled mortgages.

D. Other Government Involvement

In recent years Congress has enacted laws on a variety of other real estate finance subjects. The following statutes have had a particularly significant impact on the mortgage market.

1. Truth in Lending Act of 1968

The Truth in Lending Act (15 U.S.C.A. § 1601 *et seq.*) requires lenders to disclose financing costs and terms to prospective borrowers. As a general rule Truth in Lending applies only to consumer credit transactions involving $25,000 or less. Business or commercial loans for any amount are not covered.

Many real estate credit transactions are governed by Truth in Lending. Although business or commercial real estate loans are, of course, exempt, the Act applies to consumer real estate loans regardless of amount. The $25,000 ceiling was removed from this type of transaction so that the average home-buyer is protected when he embarks upon the only large-scale financing arrangement he may ever enter.

As a general matter, the creditor in a real estate transaction must make the usual disclosure for closed-end transactions including a statement of the amount financed, the finance charge, and the annual percentage rate. Significant differences exist, however, between his disclosure obligations and those of a creditor in a non-real estate transaction. First, the items to be included in computing the finance charge differ. Second, the real estate creditor must state whether the mortgage loan may be assumed. Third, in certain real estate credit transactions the borrower has a right to rescind that must be disclosed to

[*34*]

him. If the transaction creates a lien on the
debtor's principal dwelling that secures a non-
acquisition or non-construction loan, the consumer may rescind the transaction within three business days after closing or after the rescission
right is disclosed, whichever is later.

2. Interstate Land Sales Full Disclosure Act of 1969

Congress enacted the Interstate Land Sales
Full Disclosure Act (15 U.S.C.A. § 1701 *et seq.*) to
eliminate the use of fraudulent or misleading
practices in the marketing of certain types of raw
land. The Act applies to developers who sell or
lease unimproved subdivision lots as part of a
common promotional plan in interstate commerce
or through the mails. Numerous exemptions,
both full and partial, are available. One of the
most significant is that which exempts the developer of subdivisions containing less than 100 lots
from the Act's registration and disclosure provisions described below.

Developers covered by the Act must disclose
the material facts about the land being offered
for sale. Disclosure is accomplished by filing a
statement of record with the Office of Interstate
Land Sales Registration in the Department of
Housing and Urban Development and by delivering a property report to prospective purchasers.
The statement of record must include certain

specific information about the subdivision, the surrounding area, and the developer. The property report is a condensed more readable version of the statement of record.

The Act gives the purchaser certain remedies for the developer's failure to make proper disclosure. Rescission is available in two general instances. First, if the developer fails to give the purchaser a property report prior to the execution of a sales contract, the purchaser may rescind the contract within two years. Second, if the purchaser is furnished with a property report before he signs a sales contract, he may rescind the contract within seven days of its execution. (Frequently, the contract is an installment land contract. *See* Ch. 3, pp. 48–54. If so, additional disclosure and rescission provisions of the Act apply.)

The purchaser also has the right to obtain specific performance, damages, or other appropriate relief from the developer for violations of the Act. Although the Act does not apply to lending institutions acting in the normal course of business, a lender may be liable for damages if he actively participates in a plan to sell or lease property covered by the Act.

3. *Flood Disaster Protection Act of 1973*

Over the years large amounts of federal disaster relief funds have been paid to flood victims.

Unfortunately, a substantial portion of the money was used to rebuild structures in the same high-risk location. This situation coupled with the general unavailability of private flood insurance led Congress to establish the National Flood Insurance Program in 1968 (42 U.S.C.A. §§ 4001 *et seq.*). The Program made federally subsidized private flood insurance available to property owners in communities which established approved land use ordinances limiting construction in flood hazard areas. Few communities responded voluntarily. Thus, the Flood Disaster Protection Act of 1973 was enacted. It made participation in the Program virtually mandatory by prohibiting federally regulated lending institutions from making loans secured by mortgages on structures in flood-prone areas unless the borrower obtained flood insurance. Because such insurance is available only in communities participating in the Program, cities and town began to enact the required land use regulation. Soon flood insurance became available to property owners in most communities.

In the late 1970's the Act was amended to eliminate the prohibition against making mortgage loans on flood plain property in a nonparticipating community. But by that time, the Program had taken hold throughout the country. Moreover, federally regulated lending institutions must still require the mortgagor to obtain flood insurance when it is available.

The Program is administered by the Federal Insurance Administration. Formerly part of the Department of Housing and Urban Development, this regulatory body now operates within the Federal Emergency Management Agency.

4. *Real Estate Settlement Procedures Act of 1974*

The Real Estate Settlement Procedures Act (12 U.S.C.A. § 2601 *et seq.*), known as "RESPA," is basically a disclosure statute designed to protect homebuyers from the imposition of unanticipated, unwarranted, or excessive loan closing costs. The Act covers all "federally related mortgage loans." A mortgage loan must meet three criteria to fit within this category. First, it must be for the purchase of one to four family residential real property. Second, it must constitute a first lien on the property. Third, it must be made by or for a lender supervised by a federal agency.

When a lender receives an application for a federally related mortgage loan he must provide the prospective borrower with: (1) a copy of "Settlement Costs," a booklet prepared by the Department of Housing and Urban Development and (2) a good faith estimate of all loan closing costs. Then, at or before the closing, the lender or whoever else conducts the closing must provide both the borrower and the seller with a completed HUD–1 Uniform Settlement Statement Form setting forth the precise amount of all closing costs. The lender may not impose any fee or charge for the preparation or submission of any of the documents required by the Act.

RESPA also includes significant substantive provisions. One portion of the Act is designed to eliminate kickbacks and unearned fees. Another section limits the amount that a lender may require a borrower to place in an escrow account for the payment of insurance premiums and property taxes. *See* Ch. 4, pp. 83–84.

5. Home Mortgage Disclosure Act of 1975

As noted earlier in this chapter, one aspect of the mortgage lender's risk is whether the land offered as security is of sufficient market value to satisfy the debt in the event the borrower defaults. Some lending institutions consider all property located in a designated area of the community they serve as inadequate or high-risk collateral and, hence, unacceptable as security for a standard mortgage loan. This form of lending discrimination is known as "redlining" because of the manner in which the designated areas have sometimes been identified on a map of the community. Typically the redlined areas are older middle-class or lower middle-class neighborhoods experiencing racial transition.

The Home Mortgage Disclosure Act (12 U.S. C.A. § 2801 *et seq.*) is designed to identify and help eliminate redlining. It, however, will expire on October 1, 1985, unless extended by Congress. The Act requires depository institutions in metropolitan areas to disclose the number and amount of their residential mortgage loans by census tract or zip code. Although it makes redlining more visible, it does not provide a penalty for such activity. Congress apparently decided to rely on community pressure to force lenders to act responsibly in this area. But in this regard note that the Community Reinvestment Act of 1977 (12 U.S.C.A. §§ 2901 *et seq.*) places an obligation on regulatory agencies to determine whether a financial institution adequately serves its community and to take this factor into consideration when examining the institution or reviewing an application for a merger, a new branch, or other special action.

CHAPTER 3

REAL ESTATE FINANCING DEVICES

I. MORTGAGE

The mortgage is the most common means of real estate financing. It is both relatively uncomplicated and flexible; most states have a simple statutory mortgage form that may be expanded as the parties desire. In addition, because the mortgage is a time tested financing device, the rights and obligations of the parties are generally well established within each state.

A. Purchase Money Mortgage

The purchase money mortgage is an important mortgage species. It has been traditionally defined as a mortgage taken by the seller of real estate to secure payment of part of the purchase price. A mortgage given a third party lender as security for a loan used to acquire the mortgaged property is now also generally considered to be a purchase money mortgage.

Illustration: O contracts to sell his house to MR for $30,000. O conveys the house to MR. MR pays O $10,000 in cash and gives O a promissory note for $20,000 secured by a mortgage on the house. The mortgage is a traditional purchase money mortgage.

Illustration: O contracts to sell his farm to MR for $80,000. MR has only $20,000 cash so he obtains a $60,000 loan from ME. MR uses his cash and the loan proceeds to pay O for the farm. O conveys the farm to MR who immediately executes a mortgage on the farm to ME to secure repayment of the loan. The mortgage is considered a purchase money mortgage in most states.

It is necessary to identify the purchase money mortgage for two reasons: (1) it is the type of mortgage transaction with which the home buying public is most familiar; and (2) it receives a preferred lien priority position. *See* Ch. 9, pp. 159–161.

B. Tax Considerations

A thorough examination of the tax consequences of a mortgage transaction is beyond the scope of this book. However, the significance of federal income tax considerations in real estate finance must at least be mentioned. Ordinarily, the mortgagor receives an income tax deduction for interest paid on the mortgage loan and the mortgagee pays tax on the interest received. That is about as far as it goes in residential mortgage transactions. In commercial situations, however, tax matters are often of paramount importance. In fact, some of the financing devices discussed in this chapter were developed in large part to change the usual tax position of the parties. It is, therefore, imperative that one entering any real estate financing transaction ascertain its tax consequences at the outset, particularly in this era of constant tax reform.

II. DEED OF TRUST

The deed of trust is a form of mortgage used in many states. It is a tripartite arrangement involving the conveyance of realty by a landowner-borrower to a trustee as security for payment of the underlying obligation to the lender. The chief practical distinction between the deed of trust and the mortgage is the manner of enforcement. The deed of trust provides for foreclosure by power of sale; the mortgage usually does not. Consequently, the deed of trust is popular in those states in which out of court sale is the prevalent method of foreclosure. *See* Ch. 10, pp. 188–190.

The deed of trust is generally treated as a mortgage with a power of sale provision. The principles of mortgage law discussed in this book, therefore, are for the most part applicable to the deed of trust.

III. EQUITABLE MORTGAGES

An equitable mortgage arises whenever a court finds that an apparent nonsecurity transaction is in reality a security arrangement. There are many situations in which this may occur. Thus the maxim, "If a transaction resolves itself into a security, whatever may be its form and whatever name the parties may choose to give it, it is, in equity, a mortgage." Those transactions that commonly spawn equitable mortgages are treated in this section.

A. Absolute Deed Given as Security

A lender will occasionally require a borrower to convey property to him upon the understanding that he will hold title as security for the debt. This type of transaction is used by some lenders in an attempt to eliminate the debtor's equity of redemption and thereby avoid foreclosure. If, however, the debtor can prove that a deed absolute on its face was intended as a security device, the courts will find that an equitable mortgage was created and give the debtor an equity of redemption. Because of the strong public policy against irredeemable mortgages, the courts generally do not consider the parol evidence rule and the Statute of Frauds to be obstacles to this result.

The problem of proof is, however, a difficult matter. The key is the intention of the parties; a question upon which direct testimony is invariably at odds. The courts, therefore, look to several objective factors: the parties prior negotiations, their relative bargaining positions, the adequacy of consideration, and who is in possession of the property.

Illustration: MR, a landowner who desperately needs money, asks ME for a mortgage loan. ME responds that he will give MR $30,000 if MR will deed his property worth $50,000 to ME. MR agrees upon the condition he can continue to live on the property without paying rent. The transaction is consummated. One year later MR tenders $30,000 plus interest to ME and requests a deed to the property. ME refuses claiming complete ownership. MR's financial difficulty, his request for a loan, the amount he received, and his continued possession indicate that the parties intended the absolute deed as security for a loan. The transaction, therefore, constitutes an equitable mortgage and MR can redeem the land by paying the debt.

B. Conditional Sale

The conditional sale consists of an absolute deed coupled with an option or contract to repurchase. Again the issue is whether the transaction was intended as a security device. The same evidentiary factors considered in conjunction with the absolute deed are relevant here.

Illustration: MR, owner of a house worth $50,000, asks ME for a mortgage loan. ME requires and receives a deed of a fee simple absolute to the house. ME gives MR $30,000 and the parties enter a contract in which MR agrees to repurchase the house for $35,000 within one year. The inadequacy of consideration and MR's obligation to repurchase clearly indicate that this conditional sale was intended as a security transaction. Even if MR fails to repurchase within the time period specified, the courts will grant him an equity of redemption that ME can cut off only by foreclosure.

[45]

C. Negative Pledge

A lender may require a borrower to agree not to encumber or convey certain of his realty until a specified loan is repaid. This type of transaction is called a negative pledge. It is usually employed when the property in question is already encumbered and the lender either legally cannot take a second mortgage or chooses not to do so as a matter of customer relations. The generally accepted view is that a negative pledge does not create an equitable mortgage. The affirmative intent to create a security interest cannot reasonably be inferred from a negative promise. There is, however, some authority to the contrary.

Illustration: O owns a house which is subject to a first mortgage to ME. O obtains a loan from Bank. Bank cannot take a second mortgage on O's house, but wants O to retain the house free from other liens so that O's general financial position is not weakened. Consequently, Bank makes the loan upon the condition that O not convey or further encumber his house until the loan is repaid. If O conveys or further encumbers his house, Bank may declare its entire loan due but has no lien to foreclose. The courts generally refuse to impose an equitable mortgage in Bank's favor on the ground there was no intent to create a security device. However, in Coast Bank v. Minderhout, 61 Cal.2d 311, 38 Cal. Rptr. 505, 392 P.2d 265 (1964), the California Supreme Court found an equitable mortgage under similar circumstances.

[*46*]

D. Vendor's and Vendee's Liens

Breach of a real estate contract may give rise to a lien in favor of either the vendor or the vendee as equity requires. An equitable lien generally may be imposed for the benefit of a vendor who passed legal title to the vendee, but did not receive the entire purchase price. In some states, however, the vendor's lien is not recognized unless it was expressly reserved in the deed itself. An equitable lien also may be imposed in favor of a vendee who paid part of the purchase price, but did not receive title because the vendor breached the contract. In either case, the lien is unlike the other types of equitable mortgages discussed in this section in that it arises by operation of law not by virtue of the judicially determined intent of the parties.

Illustration: S owns a parcel of land. He enters a binding real estate contract to convey the land to P for consideration of $10,000 in cash and a $5,000 promissory note payable 30 days after closing. P gives S the cash and the note and S deeds the land to P. At the end of 30 days, P fails to pay the note. In most states, S has a $5,000 equitable vendor's lien on the land to prevent unjust enrichment. In some states, however, S does not receive a lien unless it was expressly reserved in the deed.

Illustration: S owns a parcel of land. He enters a binding real estate contract to convey the land to P. P makes a $3,000 down payment. S breaches the contract by not having a marketable title as agreed. P has a $3,000 equitable vendor's lien on

[*47*]

the property under either a trust or equitable conversion theory.

IV. INSTALLMENT LAND CONTRACT

A. Traditional Contract Approach

In a country where "pay as you go" is a way of life, it is to be expected that a financing device providing for the long term installment purchase of land would be developed. The installment land contract, referred to in some states as a contract for deed, fits the bill. It gives the purchaser possession of the land immediately, but allows him to pay the purchase price in monthly installments over a number of years. The seller retains title until all or a specific number of payments are made. The installment land contract also typically contains a time-is-of-the-essence clause and a forfeiture provision to the effect that upon default the seller may recover possession, keep the prior payments as liquidated damages, and retain title free from any rights the purchaser had under the contract. (This type of agreement for the sale of land should be distinguished from the standard real estate contract that establishes the rights of the parties pending an almost immediate transfer of title).

Because the parties to an installment land contract stand in the same relative position occupied by a mortgagor and a mortgagee, one might logically conclude that the forfeiture provision is really an illegal attempt to clog the purchaser's equity of redemption. This conclusion would be correct if the courts applied mortgage law to this financing device. The installment land contract, however, developed under contract law in which freedom of contract was the guiding principle. For this reason the installment land contract was enforced as written, forfeiture and all.

Treatment of the installment land contract as a contract, not a mortgage, caused it to become a popular means of real estate financing. It remains so today in part because some jurisdictions still follow the traditional contract approach. In these states the seller enjoys the right to recover the land upon default and retain all payments made. Foreclosure of the purchaser's interest is not required. In addition, the seller often obtains a better return on the installment land contract than on a purchase money mortgage loan and gains a tax advantage by spreading his capital gain over several years. (The seller generally may receive the same tax treatment by taking back a promissory note for part of the sale price secured by a purchase money mortgage.) Purchasers are not deterred from entering installment land contracts primarily because a low down-payment is required and many costs associated with mortgage financing are avoided.

Illustration: S owns land that P desires to purchase. Because mortgage financing funds are scarce and P cannot make a large down payment, he is unable to obtain a purchase money mortgage loan from an institutional lender. S and P, therefore, enter a typical installment land contract that provides for a 20 year term with equal monthly payments of $100. P takes possession and makes payments for 15 years. Because P is ill and out of work, he misses the first two payments in the 16th year. S declares a forfeiture. Under the traditional contract approach, S can terminate P's interest, retake possession and retain all money payments made ($18,000 out of the total $24,000 purchase price).

B. Protecting the Purchaser

There is a strong judicial and legislative trend to devise methods of protecting the purchaser from the harsh results produced by the traditional contract approach to installment land contracts. The protection afforded has taken a variety of forms. In a few jurisdictions more than one protective method is employed.

1. Period of Grace Statutes

In some states, statutes give the purchaser a period of grace to cure default before forfeiture can occur. Under these statutes the seller is often required to follow certain procedures for notifying the purchaser and terminating his interest.

2. Compelling Equities View

The courts in a growing number of states have demonstrated a willingness to examine individual installment land contracts to determine whether forfeiture is appropriate under the circumstances. This approach has been labeled the compelling equities view because forfeiture will be enforced unless the purchaser can establish reasons why it would be unjust to do so. In order to determine the reasonableness of the forfeiture in question, courts following the compelling equities view inquire into the amount of the default, the length of the default, the reason for the default, and the amount of forfeiture involved in comparison to the purchase price.

Illustration: Assume the same facts as in the immediately preceding illustration. The default was slight, of recent origin and not willful. Further, the amount forfeited was unrelated to S's actual damages. Courts in states following the compelling equities view, therefore, would not enforce the forfeiture as written. The relief granted might vary; reinstating the contract on the payment of the overdue installments, imposing a period of grace before forfeiture, or requiring foreclosure of P's interest are three likely possibilities.

3. Equitable Mortgage View

A few states recognize the installment land contract as a disguised mortgage and give purchasers an equity of redemption after default. This equitable mortgage view is significantly different from the compelling equities approach. All purchasers, not just those with substantial equities, are entitled to a foreclosure sale of their interest in the property.

4. Restitution

In some jurisdictions the courts give defaulting purchasers restitution, the right to recover payments made under the installment land contract to the extent they exceed the seller's actual damages.

5. Waiver

Courts everywhere may use the doctrine of waiver to grant the purchaser relief. If the seller has accepted late payments, he may be estopped to declare a forfeiture unless he gives reasonable notice that he intends to assert his contract rights in future cases of default.

C. Encumbering the Purchaser's Interest

The purchaser under an installment land contract may encumber his interest in the land. *See* Ch. 5, pp. 87–88. If he mortgages his interest and then defaults on the underlying installment land contract, controversy often arises between the seller and the mortgagee. The conflict centers on two issues. First, must the seller notify the mortgagee before terminating the purchaser's interest? Second, what are the mortgagee's rights after the purchaser's default?

With respect to the first issue, the general rule is that the mortgagee is entitled to notice of the impending termination of the purchaser's interest only if the seller has received notice of the mortgagee's encumbrance. There is, however, a split of authority as to when the seller is on notice of the mortgagee's interest. Some courts hold that the seller must have actual notice of the mortgage. These courts reason that the mere recordation of the mortgage is not sufficient notice to the seller because the recording statutes are designed to impart notice to subsequent purchasers, not prior interest holders. Other courts hold that the seller need only have constructive notice of the mortgage. These courts conclude that recordation of the mortgage imparts such notice to the seller because he should check the records before extinguishing another's interest. This later approach is closely analogous to the requirements imposed on a senior mortgagee who seeks to foreclose junior interest holders. *See* Ch. 10, pp. 180–182.

Assuming that the mortgagee is entitled to notice of the impending termination of the purchaser's interest, a question arises concerning his rights in the land. In at least one state the mortgagee is permitted to pay the seller the balance of the contract price and take title to the property. This approach, however, unjustly enriches the mortgagee to the extent the value of the land exceeds the total amount remaining unpaid on the installment land contract and the mortgage. Courts in other jurisdictions treat the mortgagee as a second lienor of the fee and the seller as a first lienor. In these states, the mortgagee, therefore, may either: (1) pay off the seller and be subrogated to his rights, thus becoming the holder of both the first and second liens on the property, or (2) force a sale of the property and satisfy his lien out of the sale proceeds that remain after the vendor's lien is satisfied. *See* Ch. 8, pp. 153–154; Ch. 10, p. 187. Under either alternative, the mortgagee is entitled to recover the value of his lien, but no more. This treatment of the seller and mortgagee as first and second lienors is consistent with the overall movement toward treating installment land contracts as mortgages and, hence, can be expected to gain increased support.

V. LEASE

A. Varieties

The lease plays an important part in real estate finance, particularly in the area of commercial development. Leases may be used in a variety of ways, frequently in conjunction with another financing device.

1. *Ground Lease*

The ground lease is a long-term lease employed to acquire raw land for commercial development. Its principal advantage to the lessee over outright purchase is that little or no "up-front" capital is needed and the rental payments are fully tax deductible. The ground lease and the improvements to be constructed on the property are then mortgaged to finance development. (The concept of the leasehold mortgage is discussed later in this chapter.)

> *Illustration*: D desires to develop a shopping center on O's unimproved land. D and O enter a ground lease for a 99 year term. Other lease provisions are as follows: D will complete the shopping center within a certain time period, ground rent is not payable until the center is completed, D must pay all taxes, utilities, insurance, and maintenance on the property, and all improvements belong to D until the term of the ground lease expires when they go with the land to O. D then obtains mortgage financing for the project. (As indicated in this illustration, the tenant under a typical ground lease is responsible for taxes, insurance, and maintenance. When a lease contains a provision of this type it is said to be a "net" lease because the rental income to the lessor is not reduced by payment of operating expenses.)

2. Space Lease

The financial success of many developments depends upon the developer's ability to rent the store, apartment or office space in the project. Space leases play such a significant role in the success of shopping centers and office buildings that permanent mortgage lenders generally require the developer to obtain space lease commitments from a number of substantial tenants before construction begins.

[55]

3. Acquisition Lease

In many instances a business will utilize a long term lease to acquire improved commercial property for expansion of its operations. Because this type of lease is employed as an alternative to the purchase or construction of new facilities, it is called an acquisition lease in this book.

The attraction of the acquisition lease to the lessee is much the same as that of the ground lease; small front-end cash outlay and fully deductible rental payments. The attractions, however, are somewhat stronger in the case of the acquisition lease because of the generally higher value of the leasehold being acquired.

The acquisition lease is usually a "net" lease and also often contains an escalator clause that adjusts the amount of rent to keep pace with inflation. The Consumer Price Index maintained by the Department of Labor is an economic indicator frequently used to accomplish this result. The acquisition lease, of course, is not the only type of lease in which escalator clauses are found.

B. Leasehold Mortgage

A lessee may mortgage his leasehold estate. *See* Ch. 5, p. 87. Although the discussion of mortgage law in this book concerns fee mortgages, it is generally applicable to leasehold mortgages. However, special problems arise when a mortgagee accepts a leasehold as security.

1. Nature of the Security

The principal feature of a leasehold mortgage is that the security interest of the mortgagee is subject to the rights of the lessor-owner. Consequently, many mortgagees will not make a leasehold mortgage loan unless the lessor subordinates his fee to the mortgage. The lessor may be hesitant to do so because subordination impairs his ability to borrow on his reversion and subjects the fee to sale upon the lessee's default. Nevertheless, important financial factors may cause the lessor to take this step. Subordination of the fee usually enables the lessee to obtain financing that is otherwise unavailable. Hence, the lessor may demand a higher rent and obtain more valuable property at the end of the lease term.

2. Lease Provisions

When the lease and leasehold mortgage are successive steps in one financing package, the lease is drafted to meet the requirements of the proposed mortgagee. If, however, the lease predates the mortgage negotiations, it usually is amended as specified by the mortgagee. In either case, leasehold mortgage financing presents unique problems. The areas of greatest concern to the mortgagee are treated in the following subsections of this chapter. A discussion of many other matters important to the mortgagee is outside the purview of this work.

a.　Term

The lease term should be at least as long as the mortgage term, otherwise the security will cease to exist before the mortgage debt is paid.

b.　Right to Assign, Sublet and Encumber

In the absence of a lease provision to the contrary, the lessee and his successors may encumber, assign and sublet the leasehold. The lessee's ability to encumber his estate is obviously essential to the creation of the leasehold mortgage. The lease, therefore, should not limit his rights in this regard. Also, because the mortgagee may acquire the leasehold upon foreclosure, the lease should not impose restrictions on assignment or subleasing, at least as against mortgagee.

c.　Default

Termination of the lease extinguishes the leasehold mortgage. Thus, the mortgagee usually requires that he receive notice of and the right to cure the tenant's defaults under the lease.

C.　Sale and Leaseback

The lease also constitutes part of an important financing vehicle known as the sale and leaseback. This financing technique is enormously complex in its many variations. The scope of this book permits presentation of only the basic concept.

The typical sale and leaseback is structured as follows: the owner of improved commercial property sells the property to an investor who simultaneously leases it back to the seller on a long-term, "net" basis. The reasons behind this rather puzzling transaction lie in the intricacies of business finance and federal income tax law.

The basic business finance factors are not difficult to comprehend. The owner of the property is able to obtain more capital from the sale and leaseback arrangement than from mortgage financing. Although mortgage loans are usually subject to loan-to-value limits, the sale aspect of the sale and leaseback may produce almost 100% of the current fair market value of the property. Investors are willing to provide such financing because they generally receive a higher rate of return from a sale and leaseback than from a mortgage loan. Furthermore, the return is not limited by usury statutes that apply only to loan transactions.

The general tax ramifications of a sale and leaseback are also easily understood. The seller-lessee realizes a capital gain or loss on the sale of the property and may deduct all rental payments. (Recall that only the interest portion of mortgage loan payments may be deducted). The investor-lessee receives ordinary income in the form of rental payments, but may claim depreciation deductions on the property.

The elaborate plans of the parties, however, will collapse if the transaction is found to be a security arrangement rather than a genuine sale and leaseback. Factors that tend to indicate that the transaction is really a disguised mortgage are similar to those mentioned in the section of this chapter on equitable mortgages. They include the following: the seller-lessee is financially embarrassed, the parties have not dealt at arm's length, the sale price is inadequate, the transaction, if a mortgage loan, would be usurious, and the seller-lessee is given an option to purchase for a nominal amount.

In the event the transaction is found to be a hidden security arrangement rather than a genuine sale and leaseback, disastrous consequences result. First, the parties must readjust their tax positions to reflect reality and pay any resulting tax deficiencies. Second, a question of usury may arise. Third, upon default the investor must terminate the "lessee's" interest in the property by utilizing foreclosure procedures rather than by declaring a forfeiture under the lease.

CHAPTER 4

THE UNDERLYING OBLIGATION

I. NECESSITY OF AN OBLIGATION

A mortgage is only security. It cannot exist without an underlying obligation. There is, however, no requirement that the mortgagor or anyone else be personally liable on the obligation. A mortgage transaction in which no one person has liability is known as a "nonrecourse" or "in rem" mortgage loan.

Illustration: MR executes a note and mortgage to ME. The note contains a provision that MR shall have no personal responsibility to pay the note and that ME's only remedy in event of default is to foreclose. The mortgage is valid because there is a "real" obligation that supports it.

Illustration: MR–1 executes a note and mortgage to ME. MR–1 conveys the mortgaged property to MR–2 "subject to" the mortgage. MR–2 does not assume personal responsibility to pay the note. ME then releases MR–1 from liability, but retains his rights under the mortgage. The mortgage continues unaffected by this transaction even though no one is personally liable on the note.

II. FORM OF THE OBLIGATION

A mortgage may secure any obligation that has an ascertainable monetary value. A court upon foreclosure must be able to determine the amount of the lien in order to properly disburse the sale proceeds.

> *Illustration*: ME owns 10 acres of land and agrees to sell 2 acres to MR upon the condition that MR build a sewer to service the entire original tract and consent to any applications for rezoning of the 8 acres retained by ME. MR pays the full purchase price and executes a mortgage to ME to secure the required promises. The mortgage properly secures the promise to build the sewer because the obligation is one that can be reduced to a money equivalent. The promise to consent to applications for rezoning, however, is unsecured because its monetary value is a matter of speculation. *See* Application of Jeffrey Towers, Inc., 57 Misc.2d 46, 291 N.Y.S.2d 41 (1968).

The underlying obligation my be embodied in the mortgage itself, but is usually evidenced by a separate promissory note. The promissory note may be negotiable. A statement in the instrument that it is secured by a mortgage does not destroy its negotiability. *See* U.C.C. § 3–105(1)(e). The note's negotiability is likewise unimpaired by its reference to the mortgage for rights as to prepayment or acceleration. *See* U.C.C. § 3–105(1)(c). If, however, it incorporates terms of the mortgage for other purposes, it becomes a conditional promise and is thereby rendered non-negotiable.

III. DESCRIPTION OF THE OBLIGATION

As between the mortgagor and mortgagee, it is prudent but not necessary to describe the underlying obligation in the mortgage. A description of the obligation, however, is necessary to protect the mortgagee against subsequent purchasers and lienors. Although authorities disagree regarding what information is required to impart adequate notice of the obligation, the description should specify its form, amount, date of execution and maturity. (The mortgagee, of course, must also record the mortgage. *See* Ch. 9, pp. 158–159.)

IV. FUTURE ADVANCES

A. The Basic Concept

A mortgage may secure the repayment of funds that the mortgagee advances to the mortgagor in the future. In fact, many commonly used mortgage forms contain a future advances clause. The future advance clause is also an integral part of construction loan mortgages under which the lender advances funds as construction on the mortgaged property progresses.

A mortgage that covers future advances constitutes an executory agreement by the mortgagor that the mortgaged property stands as security for all funds advanced by the mortgagee. The arrangement is one transaction, not a series of independent loans. It is specifically so designed for the convenience and economic advantage of the parties. Thus, the lien of a mortgage for future advances arises as at the date of the execution of the mortgage, not when advances are made.

B.   Methods of Securing Future Advances

The parties generally provide for coverage of future advances by drafting the mortgage in either of two ways. One technique is to specify a present loan amount in excess of funds actually advanced. A second approach is to state the amount of the current debt and then provide that the mortgage secures future advances, often without limit on the total amount secured. Both methods have been upheld by the courts, but the second alternative is more common.

C.   Obligatory/Optional Distinction

A mortgagee who holds a properly recorded mortgage for future advances receives priority over parties who subsequently acquire an interest in the mortgaged property. *See* Ch. 9, pp. 158–159. The courts, however, sometimes limit the priority of a mortgage for future advances in order to preserve the marketability of the mortgagor's title for subsequent encumbrance or sale. The necessity for limitation depends in large part upon whether the future advance is obligatory or optional.

[*64*]

1. Obligatory Future Advances

When the mortgagee is contractually obligated to make future advances, the lien for each advance has priority over all subsequent encumbrances. This is true even if the mortgagee makes an advance with knowledge that a subsequent encumbrance has attached to the mortgaged property in the interim between the execution of the mortgage and the making of the advance. No policy reason exists to change the principle that priority for future advances dates from the day the mortgage was executed. Because the mortgagor has the right to additional future advances, he is not prejudiced by the fact that he probably cannot obtain secondary financing from another lender.

Illustration: MR and ME enter a construction loan agreement that ME will advance funds up to a total of $1,000,000 as construction on the mortgaged property progresses. MR executes a $1,000,000 note and mortgage to ME who records the mortgage. ME advances $500,000 as construction progresses in accordance with the agreement. At that point MR borrows $200,000 from X and gives him a $200,000 note and mortgage. X records. ME knows of this lien, but because MR fully complies with the construction loan agreement, ME advances the remaining $500,000. ME has a first lien for $1,000,000 because he was obligated to advance the entire loan amount. X has a second lien for $200,000.

2. Optional Future Advances

Most mortgages for future advances provide that future advances are optional with the mortgagee. Mortgages for optional future advances are sometimes referred to as open-end mortgages.

a.   Priority Problems

Controversy often arises regarding the priority of optional advances over subsequent encumbrances. The outcome depends upon which of three possible fact patterns is presented: (1) The lien for optional future advances made *before* the attachment of a subsequent encumbrance clearly has priority under the fundamental principle of "prior in time, prior in right." *See* Ch. 9, pp. 158–159. (2) The lien for optional future advances made *after* the attachment of a subsequent encumbrance and *without notice* of that encumbrance also has priority on the theory that it arose at the date that the mortgage for future advances was executed. (3) The lien for optional future advances made *with notice* of the attachment of a subsequent encumbrance is generally postponed to the lien of the intervening encumbrance on the ground that the marketability of the mortgagor's land for future encumbrance or sale would otherwise be destroyed. If other lenders were unable to ensure the priority of their encumbrances over the lien of later optional future advances, they certainly would not make mortgage loans on the property. The mortgagor would then be left to the whim of the original mortgagee for additional financing.

b. The Notice Issue

The "notice" limitation on the priority of optional future advances is clouded by disagreement over the type of notice required. There are two views on the subject. The generally accepted view is that the lien of an optional future advance loses priority to the lien of an intervening subsequent encumbrance only if the mortgagee has actual notice of the encumbrance when he makes the advance. Some states, however, postpone the lien of an optional future advance to the lien of an intervening subsequent encumbrance when the mortgagee has either actual or constructive notice of the encumbrance. In these jurisdictions recording the encumbrance imparts constructive notice of its existence to the mortgagee. This approach, however, is inconsistent with established legal principles. Recording systems act prospectively only; subsequent purchasers, not prior interest holders, receive constructive notice of a recorded document. A mortgagee who makes optional future advances after an intervening encumbrance is recorded can be considered a subsequent purchaser only if the future advance is viewed as a separate loan. This is, of course, contrary to the fundamental notion that the lien for future advances arises at the date of the execution of the mortgage, not when the advance is made.

Illustration: MR borrows $20,000 from ME and gives ME a $20,000 note and mortgage. The mortgage contains an optional future advance clause and provides for a maximum total indebtedness of $30,000. ME records. MR then borrows $5,000 from X and gives X a $5,000 note and a mortgage. X records. MR next borrows an additional $10,000 from ME under the optional future advance clause in the original mortgage. The generally accepted view is that ME has a first lien for $30,000 unless he had actual notice of X's lien at the time he made the future advance. In some jurisdictions, however, ME's lien for the future advance is postponed in priority to X's lien on the ground that ME was on constructive notice of X's encumbrance. In these states, ME has a first lien for $20,000, X has a second lien for $5,000 and ME has a third lien for $10,000.

D. Obligatory/Optional Distinction Rejected by Statute

Several state legislatures have enacted statutes eliminating the distinction between obligatory and optional future advances. In these jurisdictions the lien of all future advances dates from the execution of the mortgage even if the mortgagee makes the advance with actual knowledge of an intervening encumbrance. In other words, obligatory and optional advances are treated the same; each takes priority over intervening encumbrances. Almost all of the statutes that produce this result require, however, that the mortgage specify the total amount to be secured.

E. The Construction Lender's Dilemma

The distinction between obligatory and optional future advances for priority purposes has been severely criticized by construction lenders on the ground that its application to advances made under a construction loan mortgage often produces inequitable results. Because the construction lender is obligated to make advances as construction progresses, he receives first lien priority for all advances when the project is completed according to plan. Problems arise, however, when construction does not progress smoothly and the borrower-developer defaults. Construction loan documents typically give the lender the right to stop advancing funds upon the mortgagor's default. Hence, any advances made thereafter are optional and may lose priority to intervening liens. If, however, the lender does not make additional advances, the incomplete project will probably not be of sufficient value even to cover the amount of his lien for obligatory advances made before default.

Courts often struggle to avoid the optional/ obligatory future advance rule in this situation because completion of the project enhances the value of the security for both the construction lender and any intervening lienor. Although, the hazy line between optional and obligatory advances gives the judiciary ample opportunity to exercise discretion, many judges mechanistically apply the optional/obligatory rule and conclude that advances made after default are optional. Some courts, however, award the construction lender complete lien priority if he makes post default advances in good faith and under economic compulsion. This result has long been favored by commentators and is reached by statute in those states in which the legislature has eliminated the distinction between obligatory and optional future advances.

F. Dragnet Clauses

The dragnet clause is related to the future advances clause, but is broader in scope. The typical dragnet clause, sometimes referred to as an anaconda or omnibus clause, provides that the mortgage secures all indebtedness owed by the mortgagor to the mortgagee. Every obligation is included regardless of whether it arose before or after the execution of the mortgage or whether it was originated or acquired by the mortgagee.

Illustration: MR executes a $2,000 unsecured promissory note to X. MR then borrows $5,000 from ME and executes a $5,000 note and mortgage to ME. The mortgage contains a dragnet clause. ME purchases the unsecured note from X at a discount for $1,500. ME now has a $7,000 lien on the mortgage property because both notes are fully secured by the mortgage.

Because a dragnet clause can be used to expand the amount of a lien far beyond the mortgagor's expectations, its scope has been limited by both judicial decision and legislative action. In some states application of the dragnet clause is restricted to obligations arising directly between the original parties to the mortgage. Other jurisdictions limit its application to obligations arising after the execution of the mortgage. Still other states impose various additional restrictions.

V. INTEREST

A. The Norm

The underlying obligation usually bears interest at a fixed percentage rate per annum. The precise interest rate charged is usually dictated by the money market conditions existing at the time the mortgage loan is made. But regardless of what the rate may be, it remains constant over the entire term of the loan.

B. Variations from the Norm

During periods of rampant inflation, a fixed rate of interest provides the lender with less yield than originally projected. Consequently, mortgagees have devised other methods to insure a satisfactory return on their investments.

1. *Alternative Mortgage Instruments*

The Comptroller of the Currency, the Federal Home Loan Bank Board, and the National Credit Union Administration recently authorized the federally chartered lending institutions under their control to develop alternatives to the traditional mortgage. Moreover, the Alternative Mortgage Transactions Parity Act of 1982, 12 U.S.C.A. §§ 3802–3805 (1982), preempted state law on the subject so as to permit nonfederally chartered institutions to compete effectively in the real estate financing marketplace by authorizing them to offer the same alternative mortgage instruments available from similar federally chartered institutions. The states have three years from the date of the Act to override this preemption.

As a consequence of these regulatory and legislative measures, several significant alternatives to the traditional mortgage have been developed by institutional lenders. Those innovative instruments which alter the standard fixed-interest-rate approach are discussed in this section. Newly developed mortgage formats that provide payment alternatives are treated later in this chapter.

a. Adjustable Rate Mortgage

Most mortgage lenders now offer adjustable rate mortgages (ARMs) in which the interest rate rises and falls over the term of the loan in accordance with prevailing market conditions. The market rate of interest is gauged by a predetermined index—some recognized economic indicator reflecting changes in the cost of obtaining mortgage money in the local, regional, or national market. The parties may guard against extreme interest rate fluctuations by establishing floor and ceiling limits. *See* Appendix B for an Adjustable Rate Note and an Adjustable Rate Rider to a standard mortgage.

ARMs, sometimes referred to as variable rate mortgages, may be structured in an almost infinite number of ways. Variations exist not only with respect to the index and the use of floors and ceilings, but also as to the frequency and amount of each interest rate adjustment and the way in which interest increases are paid. Moreover, an ARM may be drafted to include other flexibility features such as a graduated payment provision.

There is another noteworthy feature of some ARMs. If increases in the interest rate are added to the principal obligation rather than reflected in increased monthly payments or extended maturity, the phenomenon of negative amortization may occur. That is, over time the principal balance of the loan may increase instead of decrease.

A study recently conducted by the Federal Home Loan Mortgage Corporation reveals that

ARMs have achieved a prominent position in the mortgage financing marketplace. According to that study, ARMs constituted almost one-half of all residential purchase money mortgage loans made in the first six months of 1983. The study also found that interest rate adjustments usually were on a one, three, or five year basis and indices geared to the rate of Treasury instruments were most common.

b. Price Level Adjusted Mortgage

A residential mortgage format often used in other parts of the world to insulate lenders against inflation is the price level adjusted mortgage (PLAM). This instrument deals with the problem of inflation by tying the outstanding principal to an economic index. Thus, the interest rate remains constant over the term of the loan, but the loan principal varies. In this sense, a PLAM is the opposite of an ARM.

An advantage of the PLAM to the mortgagor is that it bears a low interest rate because inflation need not be factored into the rate of return required by the lender. On the other hand, the PLAM's primary drawback for the borrower is that it produces negative amortization which is usually covered by increased monthly payments.

c. Shared Appreciation Mortgage

Shared appreciation mortgages (SAMs) are designed to insure mortgagees of an adequate return during inflationary times and to provide an alternative form of financing for individuals who otherwise might be unable to obtain a mortgage loan. SAMs combine aspects of the standard fixed-interest-rate mortgage with a novel type of return to the lender. Typically SAMs bear a fixed-interest-rate well below current market rates thereby enabling a greater number of individuals to qualify for this form of financing than for standard fixed-interest-rate mortgages or ARMs. The SAM instrument also provides that the mortgage will receive a portion (e.g., one-third) of the amount the mortgaged property appreciates in value. The lender's fractional share of the appreciation is paid when the property is sold or at the end of a certain period (e.g., ten years), whichever comes first.

Although the SAM has appeal to both mortgagees and mortgagors, its use raises a myriad of issues: How does one determine the amount of appreciation? How are improvements made by the mortgagor factored into the calculation of appreciation? If the mortgagor does not sell the property before the lender's share of appreciation must be paid, will satisfactory refinancing be available? These and other questions cloud the SAM picture and lead authorities to draw differing conclusions regarding its future in the residential mortgage marketplace.

2. *Buy-Down Mortgage*

Mortgagees generally are willing to make below market-interest-rate loans if they receive sufficient upfront money to offset the reduced interest rate of return. A conventional mortgage loan made on this basis is called a "buy-down." Some residential real estate developers have used the buy-down technique to make their properties more marketable by paying an institutional lender to offer low-interest-rate financing to purchasers. In such case, the interest buy-down is typically for only a year or two; thereafter the interest rate returns to the market level.

3. *Equity Participation*

As a hedge against inflation, mortgage lenders sometimes demand the right to participate in the income of the project being financed. When this occurs the lender is said to receive an equity participation or "kicker." (Equity participations should be distinguished from loan participations discussed in an earlier chapter. *See*, Ch. 2, pp. 22–23.)

Several types of equity participations exist. The lender may become directly involved by entering a joint venture with the developer or by taking an ownership interest in the entity that controls the project. Probably more often the lender participates by requiring "contingent interest"—a percentage of gross income or net profit. In either case the participation usually is taken in addition to a fixed interest return.

4. *Due-on-Sale Clause*

The due-on-sale clause is commonly used by lenders to avoid being tied to low yield mortgages during periods of rising interest rates. A mortgage provision of this type gives the lender the option to accelerate the underlying obligation when the mortgagor conveys the mortgaged property. As a practical matter this enables the lender either to recover his capital for reinvestment at a higher return or to obtain an additional return on the original loan by conditioning his consent to the conveyance on the payment of a transfer fee or a higher interest rate. *See* Ch. 6, pp. 110–111.

C. Usury

The amount of interest a lender may receive is limited by state usury statutes. The provisions of these statutes vary considerably with regard to: (1) the maximum legal interest rate (2) statutory exemptions and (3) penalties for violation.

1. *Rate*

The maximum allowable interest rate on loans varies dramatically from state to state. In many states there are different maximum rates for different types of borrowers. For example, there may be one rate for individuals and another higher rate for corporations.

2.   *Exemptions*

Most usury statutes exempt certain borrowers, lenders, transactions or a combination of the three.

a.   Borrowers

Corporate borrowers are commonly exempt from usury statutes. Moreover, as previously indicated, where corporate borrowers are not exempt, they are usually permitted to pay a higher rate of interest than other borrowers. Authority is divided on the issue of whether the lender may avoid usury laws by requiring the borrower to incorporate.

b.   Lenders

Banks and savings and loan associations are exempt from usury statutes in several states.

c.   Transactions

FHA insured loans are often excluded from the application of usury laws. In addition, a purchase money mortgage loan taken by a seller of real estate is exempt in many jurisdictions on the theory that a buyer and seller are in substantially equal bargaining positions. Various other trans-

[78]

MODIFICATION Ch. 4

actions, such as loans for business purposes, are
sometimes given exempt status.

3. Penalties

In some states the penalty for usury is merely
forfeiture of interest in excess of the legal rate.
In many jurisdictions the lender forfeits all interest. In other states the lender not only forfeits
all interest but also loses the right to recover the
principal. Still other penalties exist.

4. Federal Preemption

The Depository Institutions Deregulation and
Monetary Control Act of 1980 preempted several
aspects of state usury law. The most significant
provision for real estate financing purposes is
that portion of the Act which exempts most residential first mortgage loans made after March
31, 1980, from state interest rate limits. 12 U.S.
C.A. § 1735 f–7, note (1982). The Act gave the
states the option to override this federal preemption before April 1, 1983. Several states did so.
Thus, although the Act provides some uniformity
in this area of usury law, there is still considerable diversity among the states.

VI. MODIFICATION OF THE
OBLIGATION (EXTENSION AND
RENEWAL)

A mortgage secures an obligation, not the instrument which evidences it. A change in the

[79]

form of the obligation by substitution, extension, or renewal, therefore, generally does not affect the mortgage lien. If, however, either the principal amount or interest rate is increased, the mortgage lien may lose priority to junior encumbrances to the extent of the increase.

VII. DISCHARGE OF THE OBLIGATION AND THE MORTGAGE

A. Payment

As discussed previously, a mortgage merely secures an underlying obligation. Thus, once the obligation is discharged, usually by payment, the mortgage is extinguished.

The typical modern mortgage is amortized over twenty to thirty years with provision for repayment in monthly installments of principal and interest. The amount of the mortgage lien is reduced proportionately as each monthly payment is made. When the debt is paid in full, the mortgage is discharged.

Illustration: MR executes a $25,000 promissory note and mortgage to ME. MR pays ME $15,000 on the principal of the note. The amount of the mortgage lien is reduced automatically to $10,000 irrespective of the fact the mortgage states that it secures $25,000.

1. New Payment Alternatives

Lending institutions recently were authorized to offer alternatives to the traditional payment format.

a. Graduated Payment Mortgage

Under the graduated payment mortgage, the interest rate usually remains constant throughout the life of the loan, but monthly mortgage payments increase over several years to a specified level. Initial payments are lower than normally required, whereas later payments are abnormally high. Thus, younger homebuyers may make smaller mortgage payments in their early years of employment and larger ones as their income presumably increases. This graduated payment feature may be coupled with an adjustable interest rate.

b. Reverse Annuity Mortgage

The reverse annuity mortgage allows older homeowners to borrow money on the equity in their homes. The loan proceeds are advanced to the mortgagor in monthly installments and are repaid in a lump sum at the end of a set term or when the home is sold.

c. Growing Equity Mortgage

One commonly used alternative mortgage instrument includes a fixed-interest-rate, but provides for increasing monthly principal payments so that the loan is repaid in fifteen years or so. It is from this feature that the instrument takes its name—growing equity mortgage (GEM).

Initial payments under a GEM are based on standard twenty-five or thirty year amortization. The rate of increased principal payments is specified in the document and may be fixed at a certain percentage or tied to an economic index.

2. *Balloon Loans*

Many residential mortgage loans executed before the Depression were short-term "balloon" loans upon which the borrower paid only interest until maturity. If the borrower lacked sufficient funds to satisfy the debt when it fell due, he was forced to refinance. This arrangement worked well as long as mortgage loans were readily available. During the Depression, however, money was in short supply and many borrowers were unable to refinance. Consequently, they lost their land through foreclosure. This situation caused the federal government to develop programs, notably FHA mortgage insurance, to encourage the use of the long-term fully-amortized mortgage.

Today, a balloon mortgage loan may be defined as one that requires a substantial payment at the end of the term to cover the unamortized loan principal. Disclosure of balloon payment terms is often required by regulation or statute.

3. *Escrow Accounts*

The mortgagor frequently is required to make monthly payments that cover not only principal and interest but also build an escrow account from which the mortgagee may pay real estate taxes and insurance on the mortgaged property as they come due. *See* ¶ 2 of the Standard Mortgage in Appendix A. The escrow account system originated during the Depression when many mortgagors were unable to pay real estate taxes or insurance premiums and lenders were forced to pay these obligations in order to protect their security.

The way escrow account funds are handled is usually left to the mortgagee's discretion. In the past few years, however, mortgagors in various jurisdictions have instituted class action suits contesting the legality of a mortgagee's decision not to pay interest on funds held in escrow. The mortgagors usually seek relief on one or more of the following theories: antitrust, Truth in Lending, express trust, implied trust, resulting trust, and constructive trust. Although these suits generally have been unsuccessful, the Supreme Court of Oregon granted relief on a quasi-contract/unjust enrichment theory in a case where the mortgage was silent on the question of interest. Derenco, Inc. v. Benj. Franklin Federal Savings and Loan Association, 281 Or. 533, 577 P.2d 477 (1978).

The mortgagors' attack on interest free escrow accounts has achieved greater success outside the courtroom. The controversy created by their class actions has precipitated federal and state legislative action. The federal Real Estate Settlement Procedures Act of 1974 limits the amount of funds that may be placed in escrow (*See* Ch. 2, p. 39) and statutes in some states require the payment of interest on these accounts.

4.   Late Charges

The mortgagor is often required to pay a late charge if he is tardy in making monthly payments. *See* ¶ 6(A) of the Standard Note in Appendix A. Although there is considerable division of opinion on the subject, courts generally uphold late charges calculated on a reasonable basis as nonusurious compensation to the lender for the administrative expense of handling overdue payments. In a few states, late charges are limited in amount or otherwise regulated by statute.

B.   Prepayment

The mortgagee contracts to receive interest over the agreed term of the loan. The mortgagor, therefore, has no right to pay the underlying obligation prior to maturity unless the mortgage, the note, or a local statute specifically authorizes him to do so. *See* ¶ 4 of the Standard Note in Appendix A.

> *Illustration*: MR borrows $5,000 from ME and executes a $5,000 note and mortgage to ME. The note is due 5 years from the date of execution and bears the maximum legal interest rate of 15% per annum. The instruments are silent regarding prepayment. The next day MR's father gives him $5,000. MR immediately tenders ME $5,000 to satisfy the loan. In most jurisdictions, ME may reject MR's tender and collect interest as specified in the mortgage note. Statutes in a few states, however, give MR the right to prepay even though he does not have a contractual right to do so.

Mortgages typically contain a provision giving the mortgagor the "privilege" to prepay for a fee. The fee is called a prepayment penalty and is usually specified as a percentage of the unpaid balance of the loan or as interest for a certain number of months. Although prepayment penalties are generally enforceable as reasonable compensation for lost interest, statutes in several states limit their use in residential mortgage financing. Moreover, courts are reluctant to permit the lender to collect a prepayment penalty where the mortgagor prepaid because the lender accelerated the debt under a general default provision or a due-on-sale clause.

C. Release of the Mortgage

Although the mortgage lien is automatically extinguished when the underlying obligation is satisfied, the recorded mortgage continues to cloud the mortgagor's title. The mortgagor, therefore, is entitled to a recordable mortgage release upon final payment. Mortgagees who wrongfully refuse to execute a release are subject to statutory penalties in all states.

D. Statute of Limitations

In some states the statute of limitations on the obligation is shorter than the statute of limitations on the mortgage. *See* Ch. 10, p. 180. When the statute runs on the obligation but not the mortgage, controversy arises regarding the enforceability of the mortgage. The generally accepted view is that the mortgage is still enforceable and may be foreclosed if the obligation is not paid. The running of the statute of limitations renders the obligation unenforceable, but does not discharge it. Because the obligation continues to exist, so does its security. A second view is that the remedy on the mortgage is barred with the remedy on the obligation because the mortgage is dependent on the obligation for its existence and thus also for its enforceability.

CHAPTER 5

THE MORTGAGED PROPERTY

I. MORTGAGEABLE INTERESTS

A. General

Any transferable interest in realty may be mortgaged. Thus, a fee simple, a leasehold, a life estate, a reversion, and a remainder are all mortgageable interests. Although a fee simple is the subject of most mortgages, the leasehold mortgage recently has become a popular financing vehicle. *See* Ch. 3, pp. 56–58. (The discussion in this book presumes a fee mortgage unless otherwise indicated.)

B. Mortgaging Separate Interests in the Same Land

Two or more interests in the same parcel of real estate may be mortgaged independently.

Illustration: L rents a farm to T for a 20 year term. L mortgages his reversion in fee to A Bank. T mortgages his leasehold to B Bank. Each mortgage is a valid lien on a separate interest in the farm.

C. Description

The mortgagee usually does not take possession of the mortgaged property, so he may impart notice of his lien only by recording the mortgage.

It is, therefore, imperative that the mortgaged realty be described accurately.

II.   EXTENT OF MORTGAGE COVERAGE

The mortgage lien may attach to certain property not specifically described in the mortgage.

A.   After-Acquired Property

The mortgagee may extend the mortgage lien to property subsequently obtained by the mortgagor by inserting an after-acquired property clause in the mortgage.   The clause creates an equitable lien on all property the mortgagor acquires after the execution of the mortgage.   After-acquired property clauses are often included in corporate mortgages in order to make all of the company's ever-changing property collateral for the loan.

Illustration: MR Corporation owns Blackacre. MR borrows funds from ME Bank.   MR executes a note and mortgage on Blackacre to ME.   ME records.   The mortgage contains an after-acquired property clause.   MR purchases Whiteacre as a location for a new retail outlet.   The lien of ME's mortgage automatically attaches to Whiteacre.

Because a mortgage containing an after-acquired property clause is outside the chain of title of the after-acquired property, subsequent purchasers or lienors of the property from the mortgagor will not be on record notice of the mortgagee's equitable lien.   The mortgagee, therefore,

[*88*]

must take further action to preserve the priority of his lien. Many mortgage lenders require the mortgagor to execute a recordable mortgage amendment specifically describing the after-acquired property immediately after its acquisition.

B. Easements

Easements appurtenant to the mortgaged property are part of the property and, thus, are automatically covered by the mortgage irrespective of whether they arise before or after its execution.

C. Fixtures

A fixture is an item of tangible personal property that becomes realty by virtue of its attachment to land with the intent it remain permanently affixed. The fixture concept presents two real estate finance problems.

The first issue is whether the item in controversy is a fixture. If it is a fixture, it is part of the mortgaged land and covered by the mortgage without additional description regardless of whether it became part of the realty before or after the execution of the mortgage. If the item is not a fixture, it is not part of the mortgaged land and, hence, not subject to the mortgage lien. Most mortgage transactions involve no controversy with respect to identifying fixtures. For example, the parties generally agree that a building on the property is covered by the mortgage. Moveable articles, however, present troublesome

[*89*]

questions that should be resolved by the parties at the time the mortgage is negotiated.

Even if the item in question is found to be a fixture subject to the mortgage, a second problem arises. The mortgagee must insure that the mortgage constitutes a first lien on the fixture. This issue is treated in the portion of these materials dealing with lien priorities. *See* Ch. 9, pp. 167–169.

D. Condemnation Awards

If all or part of the mortgaged property is taken by eminent domain, the mortgagee's lien attaches to the condemnation award on the theory that the award is a substitute for the land. When all the mortgaged property is taken, the mortgagee is immediately entitled to satisfy the underlying obligation out of the award. When only part of the mortgaged property is taken, authorities differ regarding the method by which the mortgagee may enforce his lien on the award. Thus, the issue of condemnation is often the subject of extensive negotiation and mortgage provision.

E. Insurance Proceeds

An insurance policy is a personal indemnification contract. Consequently, insurance proceeds are not a substitute for the destroyed property. The mortgagee, therefore, has no interest in the proceeds of a policy obtained by the mortgagor unless the policy specifically insures the interests of both parties.

F. Rents and Profits

The mortgagee may have the right to collect rents and profits from the mortgaged property and apply them to the mortgage debt. *See* Ch. 8, pp. 142–152.

III. WASTE OF THE MORTGAGED PROPERTY

A. The Doctrine of Waste

Once the mortgagee has accepted the land as adequate security for the debt, he is concerned, of course, that the mortgagor maintain the property so that it does not decrease in value. The mortgagor's duties in this regard are generally governed by the doctrine of waste, the principle that prohibits a lawful possessor from physically damaging or destroying the property he occupies.

B. The Mortgagee's Remedies for Waste

When the mortgagor commits waste, the mortgagee generally may recover damages, obtain an injunction, or commence foreclosure proceedings.

1. Damages

In title and intermediate theory states, the mortgagor is treated as a tenant liable for common law waste and the mortgagee is viewed as fictional title holder who can recover actual damages to the land either before or at foreclosure. In lien theory states the mortgagor is the owner of the mortgaged property, so he cannot commit common law waste. That doctrine applies only to acts committed by rightful possessors such as life tenants, lessees, and concurrent owners. Although in lien theory jurisdictions the mortgagee may not recover damages to the land itself, he may recover damages for the impairment of his security interest. Authorities, however, differ as to what constitutes impairment and whether an action for damages may be brought before foreclosure.

2. *Injunction*

In all jurisdictions a mortgagee may obtain an injunction against equitable waste when the mortgagor causes the property to diminish in value to the extent that the mortgagee's security is impaired. It is generally agreed that impairment in this case occurs when the property depreciates in value to a point at which the margin between the value of the land and the amount of the mortgage debt is less than prudent lenders normally require.

Illustration: MR owns property worth $11,000. MR mortgages the property to ME to secure an $8,000 note. MR cuts timber on the land that reduces it in value to $10,000. Assuming that mortgage lenders generally will not make loans in excess of 80% of the value of the mortgaged property, ME may enjoin MR from cutting more timber.

3. Foreclosure

Most mortgages contain a provision that failure to keep the property in good repair is an event of default and, therefore, a basis for foreclosure.

CHAPTER 6

TRANSFER OF THE MORTGA-GOR'S INTEREST

I. CONVEYANCE OF THE MORTGAGED PROPERTY

A. The Mortgagor's Power to Convey

The mortgagor may freely convey the mortgaged property. A mortgage provision purporting to prevent conveyance is void as an illegal disabling restraint on alienation.

B. The Effect of Conveyance on the Mortgage

When the mortgagor conveys the mortgaged property, it is important to determine whether the mortgage is discharged before title passes or survives the conveyance. The answer depends upon the contract between the mortgagor and his grantee.

1. The Mortgage is Discharged/Refinancing

The parties frequently agree that the mortgagor will pay off the mortgage debt at closing and transfer the property free from the mortgage lien. (It is presumed that the mortgage permits prepayment. *See* Ch. 4, pp. 84–85.) In this case, the purchase price is set at an amount sufficient to pay the mortgagor his equity in the property and also to satisfy the mortgage debt. If the grantee does not have enough money on hand to pay the purchase price, and he usually does not, he obtains a new mortgage loan to make up the deficit. This method of acquiring mortgaged property is termed refinancing because the existing mortgage is discharged and replaced by a new mortgage.

Illustration: MR owns a house encumbered by a $30,000 mortgage held by ME. GE agrees to purchase the property for $40,000. GE has $5,000 of his own funds and obtains a $35,000 loan from Bank. GE pays $10,000 to MR for his equity and $30,000 to ME to satisfy the mortgage debt. ME releases his mortgage and MR deeds the property to GE. GE then executes a new $35,000 mortgage to Bank. This is an example of refinancing the purchase of mortgaged property.

2. The Mortgage Survives

The parties may also agree that the existing mortgage will survive the conveyance. (Even absent such an agreement, a properly recorded mortgage will survive unless it is satisfied at or before closing. *See* Ch. 9, pp. 158–159.) In this event, the grantee pays the mortgagor the value of his equity and takes title subject to the mortgage lien.

C. Rights and Obligations of the Parties When the Mortgage Survives the Conveyance

When the mortgage survives the conveyance, the legal relationship among the mortgagee, the mortgagor and the grantee depends upon whether the grantee assumes personal responsibility for the underlying obligation.

1. The "Subject to" Conveyance

a. Grantee's Rights and Obligations

If the grantee does not assume the mortgage debt, the conveyance is merely "subject to" the mortgage. Thus, upon default the mortgagee may foreclose and have the property sold, but may not proceed against the "subject to" grantee personally.

Illustration: MR conveys mortgaged property to GE by deed that provides that the conveyance is "subject to" a prior recorded mortgage. This means that GE takes the property subject to the mortgage lien, but has no personal responsibility to pay the underlying obligation. The term "subject to" is not a promise from GE to pay the mortgage debt.

As indicated in the immediately preceding illustration, the deed from the mortgagor to the "subject to" grantee usually provides that the grantee takes title subject to the mortgage. Although a provision of this type is not necessary for the survival of a properly recorded mortgage, it is utilized by the mortgagor to limit his liability on the deed's covenants of title by excluding the mortgage from their coverage.

Illustration: MR conveys mortgaged property to GE by general warranty deed that does not mention a prior recorded mortgage. GE takes the property subject to the mortgage because he is on constructive notice of the recorded instrument. He, however, has a cause of action against MR for breach of the deed's present covenant against encumbrances.

Although the "subject to" grantee is not personally liable on the debt, he generally pays the obligation to avoid losing the property by foreclosure.

b. Mortgagor's Rights and Obligations

The mortgagor remains personally liable on the debt following a "subject to" conveyance unless he is released by the mortgagee. When he is not released, he becomes a surety, liable to the extent the land proves to be of insufficient value to satisfy the debt. As a surety he is still subject to suit by the mortgagee directly on the underlying obligation and is liable for any deficiency resulting from a foreclosure sale. If, however, he is forced to pay the entire debt, he is subrogated to the mortgagee's rights and can foreclose in order to be reimbursed to the extent of the value of the land.

Illustration: MR executes a $10,000 note and mortgage to ME. MR then conveys the mortgaged property to GE by deed which provides that title is "subject to" the mortgage. GE fails to pay the underlying obligation. ME may either (1) foreclose and seek a deficiency judgment against MR if the sale proceeds are insufficient to satisfy the debt or (2) bring suit against MR on the note without foreclosing. ME chooses the second alternative. MR pays ME $10,000 and is subrogated to ME's right to foreclose. MR forecloses and the property brings $8,000 at sale. MR is entitled to the $8,000, but he must absorb a $2,000 loss because GE had no personal liability on the note.

2.   The "Assumption" Conveyance

a.   Grantee's Rights and Obligations

A grantee taking land encumbered by a mortgage may personally assume liability for the mortgage debt. When this occurs the transaction is termed an "assumption" conveyance. Although the assumption may be accomplished outside the conveyance, it is usually based on a clause in the deed to the effect that the grantee "assumes and agrees to pay" the mortgage debt. When the grantee accepts a deed containing a clause of this type, he also accepts personal responsibility for the debt.

The mortgagor, as one of the contracting parties, may, of course, enforce the assumption contract. The mortgagee may also enforce the contract against the grantee under either of two theories. (1) The generally accepted view is that the mortgagee is a third party beneficiary to the assumption contract. (2) A few states view the mortgagee's rights against the grantee as "derived" under equitable principles from the mortgagor's rights in the assumption contract. In either case the consequence of an "assumption" conveyance is that, upon default, the mortgagee may foreclose and also obtain a deficiency judgment against the grantee. Furthermore, in most states the mortgagee may obtain judgment against the grantee on the obligation without foreclosing the mortgage. Some derivative theory states, however, refuse the mortgagee this right on the ground that the grantee is not liable on the assumption contract until the mortgagor suffers actual loss.

b. Mortgagor's Rights and Obligations

The grantee's assumption of personal responsibility for the mortgage debt does not relieve the mortgagor of liability. (*But see* p. 111 for federal regulations requiring the mortgagee to release the mortgagor in certain situations.) Again the mortgagor becomes a surety, liable for any deficiency resulting from a foreclosure sale and in most jurisdictions subject to direct suit on the debt. He is, however, in a much better position in an "assumption" conveyance than in a "subject to" transfer. First, because the assuming grantee is personally liable on the underlying obligation, he has greater incentive to pay than when he only risks loss of the land on default. Second, if the mortgagor pays the debt, he is subrogated to the mortgagee's rights and may look to both the land and the grantee personally for reimbursement. Third, the generally accepted view is that the mortgagor may sue the defaulting grantee for breach of the assumption contract without first having paid the debt.

Illustration: MR executes a $30,000 note and mortgage to ME. MR then conveys the mortgaged property to GE by deed that provides that GE assumes and agrees to pay the mortgage debt. GE fails to pay. In most states ME may either (1) foreclose and seek a deficiency judgment against MR and GE if the sale proceeds are insufficient to satisfy the note, (2) bring suit against MR on the note without foreclosing or (3) bring suit against GE on the note without foreclosing. ME chooses the second alternative. MR pays ME $30,000 and is subrogated to ME's rights against GE. MR may now either (1) foreclose and recover any deficiency from GE or (2) sue GE directly on the note and the assumption contract without foreclosing.

c. Successive "Assumption" Conveyances/ Break in the Chain of Assumptions

When successive "assumption" conveyances are made, each grantee is personally liable on the mortgage debt. The last assuming grantee, however, bears primary responsibility.

Illustration: MR executes a $20,000 note and mortgage to ME. MR makes an "assumption" conveyance to GE–1 who in turn makes an "assumption" conveyance to GE–2 who defaults. ME forecloses and receives $18,000 from the foreclosure sale. ME obtains a $2,000 deficiency judgment against GE–1. If GE–1 pays, he has the right to obtain reimbursement from GE–2.

If the chain of assumptions is broken by a "subject to" conveyance, authorities are divided on whether grantees who assume after the break are personally liable on the mortgage debt. In jurisdictions that view the mortgagee as a third party beneficiary of the assumption contract, a subsequent assuming grantee generally is liable. Some courts, however, have found the grantee free from liability on the ground that the parties did not intend the mortgagee to benefit from the assumption. In derivative theory states, a grantee who assumes after a break is not liable because the mortgagee has no claim against the "subject to" grantee and, therefore, cannot derive rights from that individual's assumption contract with a subsequent grantee.

d. Termination or Modification of the Assumption Contract

Authorities also disagree as to whether the mortgagee's rights against an assuming grantee are affected when the grantee is released from the assumption contract by his grantor. In derivative theory states, the mortgagee's rights are destroyed by the release unless he has previously filed a foreclosure suit or it would be inequitable to enforce the release against him. In most third party beneficiary theory states, the mortgagee's rights survive the release if he accepted, adopted or relied on the assumption agreement prior to the release. In a few third party beneficiary jurisdictions, the mortgagee's rights survive the release in all cases on the theory that the mortgagee's rights vested immediately upon the execution of the assumption contract.

A similar diversity of opinion exists on the question of whether the mortgagee's rights are affected by modification of the assumption contract.

3. *The Extension Problem*

The grantee normally pays the mortgage debt in both the "subject to" and the "assumption" conveyance situations. If he has difficulty doing so, the mortgagee may extend the time for payment. Serious collateral consequences may result. The extension may operate to discharge the mortgagor in whole or in part on the theory that it impairs his right as a surety to pay the debt at maturity and to be subrogated to the mortgagee's position at that time.

An extension granted an assuming grantee operates to completely discharge the mortgagor because it denies him subrogation rights against the grantee for the entire debt. Authorities, however, disagree as to the effect of an extension granted a "subject to" grantee. The generally accepted view is that the mortgagor is discharged to the extent of the value of the land at the time the extension was granted. This is because the extension costs him the opportunity to be subrogated to the mortgagee's right to foreclose.

Some states go further and completely discharge the mortgagor in this situation. Other jurisdictions consider the mortgagor's liability to be unaffected by the extension.

These rules on discharge are subject to two important qualifications. First, the mortgagor is discharged only by an extension agreement that is legally binding on the mortgagee. Mere inaction by the mortgagee after default does not constitute such an extension. Second, even when the grantee obtains a binding extension, the mortgagor is not discharged if he consents to the arrangement. Consequently, most modern mortgages provide that the mortgagee may grant extensions to subsequent grantees without affecting the mortgagor's liability.

D. Acquisition by the Mortgagee

A mortgagee may acquire the mortgaged property from the mortgagor by contract separate and distinct from the mortgage agreement. Although acquisitions of this type are not prohibited by the rule against contemporaneous clogging of the mortgagor's equity of redemption (*See* Ch. 1, pp. 4–5), they are subject to strict judicial scrutiny so that the mortgagor is protected from the generally superior bargaining power of the mortgagee. If the transaction is made in bad faith or for inadequate consideration, it will not be recognized by the courts and the mortgagor will continue to hold an equity of redemption.

1. Deed in Lieu of Foreclosure

The most common type of acquisition by the mortgagee is the deed in lieu of foreclosure. Upon default the mortgagee frequently is willing to cancel the debt and accept a deed to the mortgaged property in lieu of foreclosing the mortgagor's equity of redemption. The transaction generally is advantageous to both parties. The mortgagee avoids the expensive and time consuming foreclosure process and the mortgagor avoids a potential deficiency judgment.

2. Merger

The equitable doctrine of merger provides that when successive real property interests come into the same hands, the lesser interest merges into the greater interest and is thereby extinguished. Thus, when the mortgagee acquires the mortgaged property, the mortgage normally merges into the fee. However, because merger is an equitable doctrine predicated on the actual or presumed intention of the individual in whom the interests unite, the mortgage is preserved if merger would be detrimental to the mortgagee.

> *Illustration*: MR owns Blackacre subject to a first mortgage to ME–1 and a second mortgage to ME–2. MR conveys Blackacre to ME–1. Merger does not occur unless ME–1 expresses an intent for it to do so. It is presumed that ME–1 does not intend to gratuitously benefit ME–2 by giving his mortgage first lien priority.

II. DUE–ON–SALE CLAUSE

A. General

Although the mortgagee cannot prohibit the mortgagor from transferring the mortgaged property, he may include a provision in the mortgage giving him the right to accelerate the debt if the mortgaged property is conveyed without his consent. *See* ¶ 17 of the Standard Mortgage in Appendix A. A mortgage provision of this type is known as a due-on-sale clause. Such clauses are often broadly worded to cover the transfer of any interest in the property. Transfer by land contract, lease, or junior encumbrance, as well as by outright conveyance, are therefore acts that may trigger acceleration of the debt.

B. State Law

In the 1970's and early 1980's considerable controversy existed regarding the enforceability of due-on-sale clauses. The states were divided into two camps: those following the "automatic enforcement" approach and those subscribing to the "impairment of security" view. This split of authority was primarily the result of differing judicial attitudes as to whether the enforcement of a due-on-sale clause constituted an unreasonable restraint on alienation.

1. Automatic Enforcement Approach

Courts adopting the automatic enforcement approach generally reasoned as follows: To the extent enforcement of a due-on-sale clause directly or indirectly limits the mortgagor's ability to convey the mortgaged property, such restraint on alienation is reasonable. Mortgagees are justified in using a contractual provision to get rid of low-interest-rate loans in order to maintain their lending portfolios at or near the current market interest rate. Moreover, mortgagors in general benefit from a rule permitting mortgagees to enforce due-on-sale clauses at their discretion. The acceleration of low-interest-rate loans creates additional funds for new borrowers. It also tends to reduce the overall mortgage interest rate by alleviating the mortgagees' need to charge exceptionally high rates on new mortgage loans in order to compensate for low returns on outstanding loans.

One state court which adopted the automatic enforcement approach used markedly different analysis in doing so. It determined that due-on-sale clauses are not restraints on alienation in any sense and, therefore, are freely enforceable contract provisions. Occidental Savings & Loan Association v. Venco Partnership, 206 Neb. 469, 293 N.W.2d 843 (1980).

2. *Impairment of Security View*

Courts in a number of states found due-on-sale clauses enforceable only if the mortgagee established that the conveyance in question impaired his security interest. These courts concluded that it is unreasonable for a mortgagee to exercise a due-on-sale clause merely to improve his financial condition. Additional justification is necessary to tip the balance to the reasonable side of the scale. The grantee's present financial situation, credit history, and background respecting property use and maintenance are factors relevant to this determination.

The most analytical and best-known decision espousing the impairment of security point of view is Wellenkamp v. Bank of America, 21 Cal. 3d 943, 148 Cal.Rptr. 379, 582 P.2d 970 (1978). In *Wellenkamp* the Supreme Court of California utilized a balancing test—justification for the restraint v. quantum of the restraint—to determine the validity of due-on-sale clauses under the reasonable restraint on alienation standard.

A few other courts adopted the impairment of security view on another theory. They reasoned that it is inequitable for a mortgagee to accelerate the debt under a due-on-sale clause solely for economic reasons. The results of this approach are essentially the same as produced by the *Wellenkamp*-type restraint on alienation analysis.

C. Federal Home Loan Bank Board Regulations

In 1976, the Federal Home Loan Bank Board specifically authorized federal savings and loan associations to automatically enforce due-on-sale clauses. 12 C.F.R. § 545.8–3(f) (1982). There was some question, however, as to whether this regulation preempted restrictive state laws on the subject. The Supreme Court answered the preemption question in the affirmative in Fidelity Federal Savings & Loan Association v. de la Cuesta, 458 U.S. 141, 102 S.Ct. 3014 (1982), thereby eliminating any doubt about the authority of federal savings and loan associations in this area.

D. Garn—St. Germain Depository Institutions Act of 1982

Because of the fragmented law on the enforceability of due-on-sale clauses and the adverse economic impact of due-on-sale restrictions on lending institutions, Congress included provisions in the Garn—St. Germain Depository Institutions Act of 1982 preempting state due-on-sale law and establishing a national standard for the enforcement of due-on-sale clauses. 12 U.S.C.A. § 1701j–3 (1982). As a general proposition, the Act permits mortgagees to automatically enforce due-on-sale clauses. There are, however, two broad exceptions to this basic rule—one for "window period" loans and the other for certain transfers of residential mortgaged property.

A window period loan is one made or assumed before the enactment of the Act (October 15, 1982) in a jurisdiction which had a statewide restriction on the enforcement of due-on-sale clauses in place at the time the loan was executed or assumed. Window period loans remain subject to the restrictive state law for three years (until October 15, 1985) unless the appropriate regulatory body for the originating lender provides otherwise. Mortgage loans made by federal savings and loan associations are specifically excluded from this window period exception. This is, of course, consistent with the *de la Cuesta* decision discussed in the preceding section.

The Act also permanently excepts certain transfers of residential mortgaged property. Mortgagees are prohibited from enforcing a due-on-sale clause in nine specific residential transfer situations, including: "(1) the creation of a lien or other encumbrance subordinate to the lender's security instrument which does not relate to a transfer of rights of occupancy in the property; . . . (3) a transfer by devise, descent, or operation of law on the death of a joint tenant or tenant by the entirety; (4) the granting of a leasehold interest of three years or less not containing an option to purchase; . . . (6) a transfer where the spouse or children of the borrower become an owner of the property; . . . ." 12 U.S.C.A. § 1701j–3(d) (1982).

A final note of caution. The Federal Home Loan Bank Board is empowered to issue rules, regulations, and interpretations of the Act that apply to all lenders. 12 U.S.C.A. § 1701j–3(e)(1). The Board's activity in this area must be consulted constantly because the Act raises, but does not answer, numerous practical questions. *See* 12 C.F.R. §§ 591.1–591.6 (1984) for FHLBB action through early 1984.

E. Practical Considerations

When the mortgage contains an enforceable due-on-sale clause and the mortgagor desires to transfer the mortgaged property, the mortgagee has at least three alternatives.

(1) He may withhold consent, accelerate the debt, and then reinvest the funds at the current market interest rate. Some lenders have also sought a prepayment penalty under these circumstances, but such attempts have generally been rejected by the courts on the ground that once the lender accelerates the debt there can no longer be any *pre*payment. Moreover, the Federal Home Loan Bank Board has issued regulations under the Garn—St. Germain Depository Institutions Act of 1982 prohibiting mortgagees from charging a prepayment penalty in connection with the enforcement of a due-on-sale clause in residential transactions. 12 C.F.R. § 591.5(b)(2) (1984).

(2) The lender may consent to the transfer conditioned upon the grantee's assumption of the mortgage and the payment of a transfer fee or increased interest rate. The Garn—St. Germain Depository Institutions Act of 1982 contains an unusual provision which "encourages" the lender to consent to transfer upon the grantee's assumption of the mortgage at a blended interest rate not more than the average of the original rate and the current market rate. 12 U.S.C.A. § 1701j–3(b)(3). If, however, the lender consents to an assumption, he must by regulation release the mortgagor from personal liability. 12 C.F.R. § 591.5(b)(3) (1984).

(3) The lender may promote customer relations by consenting to the transfer without imposing any conditions.

III. FURTHER ENCUMBRANCE OF THE MORTGAGED PROPERTY

A mortgagee may place junior mortgages on the mortgaged property. *See* Ch. 2, pp. 24–25. Such further encumbrance, however, may permit mortgagee to accelerate the debt under a due-on-sale clause.

IV. TRANSFER AT THE MORTGAGOR'S DEATH

On the mortgagor's death, the mortgaged property passes to his heirs or devisees. Because the

[*111*]

mortgage debt is a personal obligation, the heir or devisee generally may compel the decedent's personal representative to pay the debt. In some states, however, statutes relieve the personal estate of this burden. In addition, specific testamentary directions regarding the payment of mortgage debts may render the general rule inapplicable in individual cases.

CHAPTER 7

TRANSFER OF THE MORTGA-GEE'S INTEREST

I. THE MORTGAGEE'S INTEREST

The legal problems that arise from the transfer of the mortgagee's interest are some of the most complicated and confusing ones in real estate finance. This is primarily because the mortgagee's interest in the mortgage loan consists of two types of property, the obligation which is personalty and the mortgage which is realty. The material in this chapter is more easily understood if the reader keeps this duality constantly in mind.

II. ASSIGNMENT OF THE MORTGAGE LOAN

A. The Basic Concept

A mortgage cannot be transferred except in connection with the transfer of the obligation it secures. *See* Ch. 1, pp. 1–2. This principle has two facets. First, when the mortgagee assigns only the underlying debt, the mortgage is automatically carried to the assignee as an inseparable incident of the debt. The assignee may then require the mortgagee to execute a formal mortgage assignment. Second, when the mortgagee assigns only the mortgage, the transaction is

invalid and the assignee acquires no interest in
either the mortgage or the debt. If, however, the
mortgagee intends the separate mortgage assignment to operate also as an assignment of the
secured indebtedness, the transfer is valid and
the assignee receives an equitable right to the
debt.

Illustration: MR executes a note and mortgage
to ME. ME assigns the note to A who purchases it
without knowledge that it is secured by the mortgage. Nonethless, A has an equitable right to the
mortgage. ME holds the mortgage in trust for A
and must transfer it to A upon request.

Illustration: MR executes a note and mortgage
to ME. ME assigns the mortgage to A, but keeps
the note under the mistaken belief that both he and
A have rights against MR. The attempted transfer
is ineffective. A acquires no interest in the mortgage loan.

Illustration: MR executes a note and mortgage
to ME. ME gives the note to his attorney X for
safekeeping. Later ME requests X to return the
note so that he can transfer it to A. X refuses on
the ground that ME has failed to pay him for legal
services rendered. ME is undeterred and assigns
the mortgage to A with the express intention that
the assignment also operate as an assignment of the
note. The assignment is effective. A may enforce
both the note and the mortgage subject to X's lien
right, if any.

The usual transfer of a mortgage loan involves
separate assignments of the obligation and the
mortgage. The validity of the assignment of the

obligation is governed by the law of contracts and commercial paper. The formal assignment of the mortgage must comply with the requirements for the conveyance of an interest in land.

B.   Rights of the Assignee

The assignee of a properly transferred note and mortgage is entitled to receive payment of the debt and to foreclose the mortgage in the event of default.

C.   Recording the Assignment

The assignee must record the mortgage assignment in order to preserve his interest against subsequent purchasers or encumbrancers of the mortgaged property. *See* Ch. 9, pp. 158–159.

Illustration: MR owns land worth $20,000. MR executes a $10,000 note and mortgage on the property to ME. ME assigns and delivers the instruments to A, but A does not record. ME and MR enter into a scheme to defraud A. ME executes a release of the mortgage to MR who records it. MR then conveys the land to X, an innocent purchaser, for $20,000, an amount that is twice as much as MR normally could have obtained. *See* Ch. 6, pp. 94–95. X owns the land free from the mortgage because the record did not reflect A's current lien on the property. A's only recourse is against MR and ME.

D.   The Secondary Mortgage Market

The assignment process occurs thousands of times each day. Many mortgagees originate mortgage loans and then sell and assign them to permanent investors. The aggregate of these assignment transactions constitutes the secondary mortgage market. *See* Ch. 3, pp. 32–33.

III. DEFENSES AVAILABLE AGAINST THE ASSIGNEE

The general rule is that the holder of a mortgage loan can enforce the mortgage only to the extent that he can enforce the underlying obligation. This doctrine is based on the fundamental concept that the obligation is the principal aspect of the transaction and the mortgage is just an appendage. The form of the obligation, therefore, is of primary importance in determining what defenses the mortgagor may assert against an assignee of the mortgage loan.

A. Nonnegotiable Obligation

If the underlying obligation is nonnegotiable, the assignee takes the note and the mortgage subject to all defenses the mortgagor has against the mortgagee.

Illustration: ME agrees to loan $3,000 to MR. MR executes a $3,000 nonnegotiable note and a mortgage to ME. ME, however, does not actually advance any money to MR. ME immediately assigns and delivers the instruments to A, who is a bona fide purchaser for value without notice of ME's failure to advance funds. MR refuses to pay A. A cannot recover on the note nor can he foreclose the mortgage, he took the instruments subject to MR's defense of failure of consideration.

B. Negotiable Obligation

If the underlying obligation is negotiable and the assignee is a holder in due course (One who obtains the note for value, in good faith, and without notice it is overdue or of any defense or claim to it. *See* U.C.C. § 3–302(1).), the assignee takes the note *and* mortgage free from personal defenses the mortgagor had against the mortgagee. Personal defenses include failure of consideration, non-delivery, payment, and fraud in the inducement. *See* U.C.C. § 3–306.

This negotiable mortgage concept rests on the theory that negotiable notes should be freely transferable and that the mortgage, as mere security, should travel with the note. A few jurisdictions, however, reject this principle on the ground that a mortgage is a property interest for all purposes and thus cannot assume the characteristics of commercial paper. Under this minority approach, even a holder in due course takes the mortgage subject to personal defenses the mortgagor has against the mortgagee.

Illustration: ME agrees to loan $3,000 to MR. MR executes a $3,000 negotiable note and mortgage to ME. However, ME does not actually advance any money to MR. ME immediately negotiates, assigns and delivers the instruments to A, a holder in due course. As a holder in due course, A takes the note free from any personal defenses MR had against ME. The defense of failure of consideration is a personal defense. A, therefore, may recover $3,000 on the note from MR. In a vast majority of states, A may also foreclose on the theory that the mortgage is clothed with the negotiable characteristics of the note and thus, A also takes that instrument free from personal defenses. In a few jurisdictions, A cannot foreclose on the ground that a mortgage can never become negotiable and therefore, MR can assert his personal defense in a foreclosure suit.

Even if the assignee qualifies as a holder in due course, he still takes subject to "real" defenses the mortgagor has on the negotiable obligation. Real defenses include incapacity, duress, infancy and fraud in the fact. *See* U.C.C. § 3–305(2).

   Illustration: Assume the same fact situation as in the immediately preceding illustration except MR alleges and proves he was insane at the time he executed the note and mortgage. Even though the note is negotiable and A is a holder in due course, A takes the note subject to the real defense of incapacity. Because MR has a valid defense against enforcement of the negotiable note, he also has a defense against enforcement of the mortgage. Thus, A can neither recover on the note nor foreclose.

Of course, if the assignee does not qualify as a holder in due course, he takes the note and mortgage subject to both real and personal defenses the mortgagor had against the mortgagee.

C. Estoppel Certificate

Many assignees will not accept an assignment unless they receive an estoppel certificate from the mortgagor setting forth the unpaid balance of the obligation and stating that he (the mortgagor) claims no defenses against the mortgagee-assignor. The assignee may thereby protect himself from all defenses, whether real or personal.

IV. PAYMENT PROBLEMS

The assignee of a mortgage loan is entitled to receive all payments made after the assignment. Nonetheless, the mortgagor or his grantee may continue to pay the original mortgagee through inadvertence or ignorance. In most instances the original mortgagee merely forwards the payment to the assignee and the parties eventually work out the administrative details. Problems arise, however, when the original mortgagee absconds with the funds or becomes insolvent. Who bears the loss, the payor or the assignee? In order to answer this question, one must ascertain who made the payment (the mortgagor or a grantee), the form of obligation involved (negotiable or nonnegotiable) and the type of payment made (part or final). Because the mortgage is a mere incident of the obligation, commercial paper law generally dictates the outcome. The result is not always consistent with the policy underlying the recording statutes.

A. Payment by the Mortgagor

1. *Negotiable Obligation*

If the underlying obligation is negotiable, the generally accepted view is that the mortgagor pays the original mortgagee at his peril. Proper payment, whether part or full, can be made only to the holder of a negotiable instrument. *See* U.C.C. § 3–603. The mortgagor is protected in that he has the right to demand production of the instrument and its surrender if the payment is final, or an endorsement thereon of part payment if that is the case. If, however, the holder is not a holder in due course and the mortgagor paid the original mortgagee without notice of the prior assignment, the mortgagor may be able to successfully assert the contract defense of payment against the holder. *See* U.C.C. § 3–306(b). (The issue of notice is discussed in the following subsection on nonnegotiable obligations.)

In a handful of states, statutes authorize the mortgagor to pay the mortgagee until an assignment of the mortgage is recorded. Such statutes, of course, run contrary to basic commercial paper policy stated above.

The severity of the general rule that the mortgagor must pay the holder of a negotiable instrument is softened by the realities of mortgage financing. Often the assignee of the negotiable note and mortgage will authorize the mortgagee to "service" the loan. *See* Ch. 2, pp. 14–15. The mortgagee thereby continues to collect payments as agent for the assignee. Naturally such payments are good against the servicing agent's principal—the holder of the negotiable note.

2. *Nonnegotiable Obligation: The Notice Problem*

If the underlying obligation is nonnegotiable, the mortgagor may safely pay the mortgagee until he receives notice of an assignment. He may receive notice in various ways.

a. Actual Notice

The mortgagor may receive actual notice of the assignment from the assignor, the assignee, or otherwise. Most assignees notify the mortgagor of the assignment as a matter of routine.

b. Constructive Notice

The recordation of a mortgage assignment generally is not constructive notice to the mortgagor because recording imparts notice only to subsequent purchasers, not to prior interest holders.

c. Inquiry Notice

In some states, the mortgagor receives inquiry notice of an assignment if upon final payment the mortgagee does not produce and surrender the note or give a reasonable excuse for his inability to do so. This view is based on the belief that it is simply prudent business practice for the mortgagor to demand production of a nonnegotiable note when he pays it off. In other jurisdictions, the mortgagor is not on inquiry notice of an assignment when the mortgagee fails to produce the note upon final payment. This view is supported by the fact that the assignee could have easily protected himself by notifying the mortgagor of the assignment.

The mortgagor's part payment of a nonnegotiable obligation is viewed in a different light. It is not common business practice to require production of a nonnegotiable note upon part payment. The mortgagor, therefore, is not on inquiry notice of an assignment just because the mortgagee fails to produce the instrument each time an installment payment is made.

B. Payment by a Grantee

When the mortgagor transfers the mortgaged property to another party, additional payment problems arise.

1. Negotiable Obligation

If the mortgage expressly secures a negotiable instrument, the grantee must pay the holder of the note. He cannot safely pay the mortgage owner of record because commercial paper law makes a negotiable instrument freely transferable. He, therefore, must demand production of the note before making either part or full payment. However, the defenses discussed above in connection with payment by the mortgagor also may be available to the grantee.

2. *Nonnegotiable Obligation: The Notice Problem*

If the underlying obligation is nonnegotiable, the grantee may pay the mortgagee until he receives notice of an assignment. Again notice may come from several different sources.

a. Actual Notice

The grantee may receive actual notice of the assignment from the mortgagor, the assignor, the assignee, or otherwise.

b. Constructive Notice

The grantee also may receive notice from the public records. A properly recorded mortgage assignment is constructive notice to a subsequent grantee.

Illustration: MR executes a nonnegotiable note and a mortgage to ME. ME assigns and delivers the instruments to A who records the mortgage assignment. MR then sells and conveys the mortgaged property to GE subject to the mortgage. GE has no actual knowledge of the assignment, so he makes part payment to ME. The payment is not good against A. GE was on constructive notice of A's interest because the records reflected the assignment at the time he purchased the mortgaged property.

c. Inquiry Notice

The grantee generally may receive inquiry notice of an assignment in the same fashion as the mortgagor. Thus the discussion of inquiry notice found in the subsection on payment by the mortgagor is equally applicable here.

V. CONFLICTING ASSIGNMENTS

An unscrupulous mortgagee may sell and assign the mortgage loan to two or more parties. The conflict among these assignees is not easily resolved.

A. Nonnegotiable Obligation

If the underlying obligation is nonnegotiable, priority among the assignees is governed by applicable recording statutes. This means that the first assignee prevails unless a subsequent assignee fits within the protection afforded by the statutes. *See* Ch. 9, pp. 158–159.

> *Illustration*: MR executes a nonnegotiable note and mortgage to ME. ME sells, assigns and delivers the instruments to A–1 who records the mortgage assignment. ME then sells and assigns to A–2, but, of course, cannot deliver the instruments. A–1 and A–2 each claim ownership of the mortgage documents. A–1 prevails over A–2, because A–2 received constructive notice of A–1's prior assignment from the record. He also received inquiry notice from ME's failure to deliver the instruments.

B. Negotiable Obligation

If the underlying obligation is negotiable, the generally accepted view is that commercial paper law, not the recording statutes, determines the rights of the competing assignees. Hence, the assignee who takes possession of the instruments generally prevails.

Illustration: MR executes a negotiable note and mortgage to ME who records. ME sells and assigns the loan to A–1, but retains possession of the instruments. A–1 records the mortgage assignment. ME then sells, assigns and delivers the instruments to A–2 who takes in good faith without actual notice of the prior assignment. A–1 and A–2 each claim ownership of the note and mortgage. Under the generally accepted view A–2 prevails over A–1 because constructive notice from the records does not prevent him from becoming a holder in due course, actual notice is required.

Illustration: MR executes a negotiable note and mortgage to ME. ME sells and assigns the note and mortgage to A–1 who takes possession of the instruments, but does not record the mortgage assignment. ME then sells and assigns the instruments to A–2 who relies on the record, but, of course, does not receive the instruments. A–1 and A–2 each claim ownership of the note and mortgage. Under the generally accepted view A–1 prevails because A–2 is not a *holder* in due course and, therefore, takes subject to A–1's claim of legal title.

VI.   FRACTIONAL ASSIGNMENTS (LOAN PARTICIPATIONS)

A.   Forms of Loan Participations

Mortgagees frequently assign fractional interests in large mortgage loans to other investors. This technique is referred to as loan participation. *See* Ch. 2, pp. 22–23. A loan participation is generally structured in either of two ways. (1) The mortgagee takes a single mortgage note from the mortgagor, holds it and issues participation certificates to the investors. (2) The mortgagee takes a series of notes from the mortgagor, each one for a fractional part of the mortgage debt. He then assigns some of the notes to the investors.

The series of notes method of participation was formerly quite common, but today the certificate approach is used almost exclusively. In either case, priority problems arise when the foreclosure sale proceeds are insufficient to pay all the investors.

B.   Agreement Establishing Priority

Most modern participations are governed by a separate participation agreement that establishes priority among the parties. (An agreement regarding priority, of course, could be included in the mortgage.) The agreement usually provides that all investors, including the mortgagee, have equal priority and share ratably in the foreclosure sale proceeds.

C. Priority Absent Agreement—Series of Notes

Participations originally involved the assignment of a series of notes. The parties to these participations often failed to make provision in the mortgage for priority among the holders of the notes. Absent such an agreement, the courts were forced to develop principles governing the allocation of foreclosure sale proceeds. A tangle of conflicting rules and exceptions resulted.

1. Pro Rata Rule

The general rule is that, absent agreement fixing priority, the mortgage is enforced on a pro rata basis in favor of the mortgagee and all assignees. This rule is predicated on the theory that equality is equity.

> *Illustration*: MR executes five $1,000 notes and a mortgage to ME. ME sells and assigns one note to each A, B, C and D. ME retains one note. The parties make no agreement regarding the priority of their interest. MR defaults and foreclosure sale produces $2,000. Under the pro rata rule each ME, A, B, C and D is entitled to ⅕ of the $2,000 proceeds ($400).

a. The Guaranty Exception

Courts in most pro rata states make an exception to the general rule when the mortgagee assigns a note by unqualified endorsement or with a guaranty of payment. In those cases, the assignee is generally awarded priority over the mortgagee on the theory that he has the greater equity.

b. The Priority for Assignees Exception

In a few pro rata jurisdictions, the general rule is not available to the mortgagee. The note or notes he retains are postponed in priority to those held by the assignees.

Illustration: Assume the same fact situation as in the immediately preceding illustration. In a state that applies the pro rata rule only to assignees, A, B, C and D have a $4,000 first lien as a group and ME has a $1,000 second lien. Each assignee receives ¼ of the $2,000 proceeds obtained at foreclosure ($500). ME recovers nothing because the proceeds are not sufficient to pay off the assignees' $4,000 first lien.

Priority for assignees is justified on a variety of equitable grounds that have a common source, the theory that assignment of part of the debt operates also as a pro tanto assignment of the mortgage lien. Thus, the priority for assignees exception to the pro rata rule is sometimes inaccurately referred to as the pro tanto rule. The label is misleading because the pro tanto assignment concept is applied only between the mortgagee and the assignees. The assignees themselves share pro rata. The priority for assignees exception is, therefore, at most a severely limited pro tanto approach. As discussed later in this chapter, the true pro tanto rule establishes priority among assignees in the order they acquire their notes.

c. The Order of Maturity Exception

Some pro rata states do not apply the general rule if the mortgage debt is represented by a series of notes having different dates of maturity. In these states priority is awarded the parties in the order of maturity of their notes.

Illustration: MR executes to ME a series of three $1,000 mortgage notes: # 1 matures in one year, # 2 matures in two years and # 3 matures in three years. The notes are all secured by a single mortgage. ME sells and assigns note # 1 to A and note # 2 to B. The parties make no agreement regarding the priority of their interests. MR defaults and a foreclosure sale produces $1,500. Under the order of maturity exception, A receives $1,000, B receives $500 and ME receives nothing.

2. *Priority of Assignment Rule (Pro Tanto Rule)*

A few jurisdictions reject the pro rata rule with its various exceptions in favor of the principle that, absent agreement to the contrary, assignees have priority in the order the assignments were made. This approach, known as the priority of assignment rule or the pro tanto rule, is based on the theory that each assignee receives so much of the mortgage as is necessary to satisfy the interest assigned. Under this approach subsequent participants take subject to the rights of prior assignees and the mortgagee takes subject to all.

   Illustration: MR executes to ME a series of three $1,000 notes maturing in three successive years. The notes are secured by a single mortgage. ME assigns one of the notes to A and then assigns another note to B. The parties make no agreement regarding the priority of their notes. MR defaults and foreclosure sale produces $1,500. Under the pro tanto rule, A receives $1,000, B gets $500 and ME receives nothing. The maturity dates of the notes are irrelevant.

D. Priority Absent Agreement—Participation Certificates

Participations are now usually formed by the use of participation certificates. Priority among the investors is almost invariably covered by a participation agreement. In the rare instances where no agreement exists, the pro rata rule applies because the certificates do not purport to assign any specific part of the mortgage loan. Thus, absent an agreement to the contrary, all investors, including the mortgagee, hold undivided interests having equal priority.

There is one exception to this rule. If the mortgagor guarantees payment of a certificate, the certificate holder is given priority over the mortgagee on the ground the guaranty indicates an intent to grant him a superior claim.

VII. ASSIGNMENT BY OPERATION OF LAW (SUBROGATION)

The courts may imply an assignment of the mortgage by operation of law under the equitable doctrine of subrogation. In real estate finance law, subrogation is the substitution of one who pays the mortgage debt to the position of the mortgagee.

A. Individuals for Whom Subrogation is Available

A payor who is neither the primary obligor nor a mere volunteer may be subrogated to the rights of the mortgagee. (The primary obligor and the volunteer are not eligible for subrogation because they have no compelling equities in their favor.) Following are four situations in which the payor commonly qualifies for this form of equitable relief.

1. *Mortgagor As Surety After Conveyance*

When the mortgagor conveys the mortgaged property subject to the mortgage, he becomes a surety. *See* Ch. 6, pp. 95–100. If the grantee fails to pay the obligation and the mortgagor is forced to do so, justice demands that the mortgagor be subrogated to the rights of the mortgagee.

Illustration: MR executes a note and mortgage to ME. MR sells and conveys the mortgaged property to GE subject to the mortgage. GE fails to pay the obligation, so MR as surety pays ME. MR is thereby subrogated to ME's right to foreclose. If GE assumed the obligation, MR also receives ME's right to recover a deficiency judgment against GE.

2.   *Junior Mortgagee*

When a junior mortgagee pays off a prior lien for the protection of his own security interest, he is subrogated to the rights of the mortgagee receiving payment.

Illustration: MR executes a $10,000 note and mortgage to ME–1. MR then executes a $5,000 note and second mortgage on the same property to ME–2. MR becomes insolvent and defaults on both obligations. Property values have recently slumped and it is projected that a foreclosure sale will produce only $10,000. Because ME–2 will receive nothing in that case, he desires to postpone foreclosure. He, therefore, pays ME–1 and is subrogated to ME–1's rights. The land remains subject to two liens, both in favor of ME–2 who can wait until property values rise to foreclose.

3.   *Lender of Pay off Funds*

One who loans funds to pay off an existing mortgage may be subrogated to the rights of the mortgagee receiving payment.

Illustration: MR executes a note and mortgage to ME. MR obtains a loan from L to pay off ME and executes a new note and mortgage to L. MR uses the loan proceeds to pay ME. L's mortgage, however, is defective for some reason. L is subrogated to ME's rights in order to cure the defect and give him the security for which he bargained.

Illustration: ME–1 holds a first mortgage on MR's land and ME–2 holds a second mortgage. MR borrows money from L to pay off ME–1. L is ignorant of ME–2's mortgage even though it is recorded. MR executes a note and mortgage to L. MR uses the loan proceeds to pay ME–1. L then discovers ME–2's mortgage lien. The courts in most jurisdictions will subrogate L to ME–1's priority position on the theory that equity demands it and ME–2 is not prejudiced. Courts in a few states, however, refuse to apply the doctrine of subrogation because L's loss was the result of his own negligence in failing to check the records.

4. Purchaser of the Mortgaged Property

When a purchaser of the mortgaged property assumes and pays the mortgage debt under the mistaken belief that no junior encumbrances exist, he is generally subrogated to the rights of the mortgagee.

Illustration: MR owns Blackacre subject to a first mortgage to ME–1 and a second mortgage to ME–2. MR sells and conveys Blackacre to GE who assumes the obligation to ME–1. GE is ignorant of ME–2's mortgage even though it is recorded. If GE pays ME–1, he is generally subrogated to ME–1's priority position in order to prevent the gratuitous advancement of ME–2's lien priority.

B. Conventional Subrogation

The mortgagor and the payor sometimes enter an agreement that subrogation should occur in the payor's favor. Although subrogation consistent with this agreement is called conventional subrogation, the actual legal effect of the agreement is subject to dispute. Some courts treat conventional subrogation as solely contractual in nature and, therefore, separate from equitable subrogation. (Equitable subrogation is sometimes referred to as legal subrogation.) Many courts, however, view the agreement calling for subrogation as merely an important factor that often influences equity to act to prevent injustice in individual cases.

Illustration: MR obtains a construction loan from ME and executes a note and mortgage to ME. During the course of construction M performs work on the project, but is not paid. Under state law, M may file a mechanics lien on the property within ninety days after completion of the project. The lien will relate back to the date of commencement of construction. *See* Ch. 9, pp. 169–171. ME's construction loan mortgage was recorded prior to commencement of construction, and, thus, under state law has priority over all mechanics liens. Sixty days after completion of construction, P makes a permanent mortgage loan to MR to "take-out" ME's construction mortgage loan. *See* Ch. 2, pp. 11–12. MR executes a new note and mortgage to P. The mortgage contains a provision that P is subrogated to any lien discharged by proceeds of P's loan. Eighty days after completion of construction, M records a mechanics lien that relates back to the date of construction and, therefore, is prior to the lien of P's mortgage. P, however, is subrogated to ME's priority position in all states, but on different theories.

In some jurisdictions subrogation is enforced as a contractual right. In others subrogation occurs by operation of law on the theory that the existence of the agreement indicates that P is entitled to equitable relief.

C. Compelling a Formal Assignment

A subrogee usually can compel the mortgagee to formally assign the obligation and the mortgage.

VIII. TRANSFER AT THE MORTGAGEE'S DEATH

The mortgagee's interest in the mortgage loan passes as personal property at his death on the theory that the mortgage, the realty aspect of the mortgage loan, is merely an incident of the obligation, the personalty aspect. This rule is, however, of waning significance. Two reasons exist for its decline. First, most mortgagees are corporations that may last in perpetuity. Second, even when the mortgagee is an individual, modern intestacy statutes generally provide that personalty and realty descend in the same way.

CHAPTER 8

RIGHTS AND DUTIES AFTER DE-
FAULT AND BEFORE
FORECLOSURE

I. DEFAULT

A. Definition and Significance of Default

Default occurs when the mortgagor fails to pay the underlying debt or to perform some other obligation secured by the mortgage. What constitutes default in each case, therefore, can be determined only by examining the mortgage documents in question.

Default activates a set of mortgage law principles that determine the rights and duties of the parties until foreclosure occurs. This chapter is devoted to an analysis of these principles.

B. Common Types of Default

1. Failure to Pay Principal and Interest

Most defaults occur as a result of the mortgagor's failure to pay monthly installments of principal and interest.

2. Failure to Pay Taxes or Insurance

The mortgagor's failure to pay taxes or insurance premiums once were common types of default. The use of escrow accounts, however, has reduced the frequency of defaults in these areas. *See* Ch. 4, p. 83.

3. Waste

Most mortgages provide that the commission of waste on the mortgaged property constitutes default. *See* Ch. 5, pp. 91–93.

4. Construction Difficulties

Construction mortgages present special possibilities for breach. Default often occurs because the mortgagor is unable to complete the contemplated improvements in accordance with the terms of the construction loan agreement. *See* Ch. 2, pp. 12–13.

C. Waiver of Default

The mortgagee may waive default by accepting late payment or other tardy performance. Lenders are usually willing to make some allowance for the borrower's financial difficulties because a modicum of tolerance often reaps greater monetary return than hasty invocation of expensive and time-consuming foreclosure procedures.

Waiver of one late performance traditionally has not been viewed as constituting waiver of subsequent late performances. Some courts, however, may require a mortgagee accepting late performance to give the mortgagor notice of his intention to require timely performance in the future. Many modern mortgages address this subject by providing that forbearance does not constitute waiver. *See* ¶ 10 of the Standard Mortgage in Appendix A. Mortgage clauses permitting the mortgagee to assess a charge for late payment are also common. *See* Ch. 4, p. 83.

II. ACCELERATION

A. The Acceleration Clause

One of the most important clauses in the modern amortized mortgage is that provision authorizing the mortgagee to accelerate the entire debt when the mortgagor defaults in the payment of a single monthly installment or in the performance of any other obligation secured by the mortgage. *See* ¶ 19 of the Standard Mortgage in Appendix A. Without an acceleration clause, the mortgagee can institute foreclosure proceedings to recover only the amount in default. Further, if he does foreclose, authorities are in conflict as to whether the lien for the amount not in default survives foreclosure.

> *Illustration*: MR executes a $40,000 note and mortgage to ME. The documents provide for equal monthly payments of $300 over a 30 year term, but do not include an acceleration clause. MR misses 2 payments. ME may institute foreclosure proceedings, but is only entitled to that part of the proceeds sufficient to satisfy the partial default ($600). In many states, the mortgage lien continues on the property to secure the unpaid balance of the debt. Any surplus goes to the mortgagor. In some juris-

dictions, however, the property is sold free from the mortgage lien. In such case, the surplus is usually either applied immediately to the unpaid balance of the loan or placed in trust to cover the debt as it matures.

B. Acceleration Clause Omitted From Either the Note or the Mortgage

The same acceleration clause should be inserted in both the note and mortgage. If it is omitted from either, the mortgagee may experience difficulty in accelerating the loan. Authorities are divided concerning the significance of the omission. One view is that the mortgagee can accelerate under both documents on the ground the note and mortgage are integral parts of one contract. The other view is that the mortgagee can only accelerate under the document containing the acceleration clause.

Illustration: MR executes a note and mortgage to ME. The mortgage contains an acceleration clause, but the note does not. MR defaults by failing to make 2 monthly payments. ME can accelerate under the mortgage and foreclosure for the full amount of the debt. In some states ME also can obtain a deficiency judgment against MR on the note. In others, he cannot.

C. Triggering Acceleration

Acceleration clauses are usually activated at the mortgagee's option. A self-operating clause could result in acceleration contrary to the mortgagee's best interest. Optional acceleration is triggered by the mortgagee's performance of an act that clearly evidences his intent to treat the entire debt due. In most states, formal notice of acceleration is unnecessary. The filing of a foreclosure complaint is generally sufficient to indicate an election to accelerate. Today, however, many mortgages contain provision requiring the mortgagee to mail notice of acceleration to the mortgagor. *See* ¶ 19 of the Standard Mortgage in Appendix A.

D. Curing Default Before Acceleration

The mortgagor may reinstate the mortgage loan by curing the default before the mortgagee elects to accelerate.

> *Illustration*: MR executes a note and mortgage to ME. The documents contain identical optional acceleration clauses. MR defaults by missing one monthly payment. If MR makes late payment to ME before ME accelerates, the loan is reinstated and ME may not use the cured default as a basis for acceleration. He, of course, may accelerate after a later default.

E. Curing Default After Acceleration

1. *General Rule*

After the mortgagee elects to accelerate, the general rule is that the mortgagor cannot reinstate the loan by curing the original default. He must pay the entire debt or face foreclosure. Recently, however, several state legislatures have enacted statutes that permit residential mortgagors to nullify acceleration by just paying the amount originally in default. Moreover, some commonly used mortgage forms now give the mortgagor a similar contract right. *See* ¶ 18 of the Standard Mortgage in Appendix A.

2. *Equitable Relief*

Mortgagors occasionally seek to have an acceleration set aside on the ground the default which triggered it resulted from misunderstanding or excusable neglect. Equitable relief is generally unavailable because most courts view the acceleration clause as simply an agreement setting a time for payment that involves neither a forfeiture nor a penalty. In a growing number of jurisdictions, however, the courts refuse to recognize an acceleration that would produce an inequitable or unjust result.

Illustration: MR executes a note and mortgage to ME. The documents contain identical optional acceleration clauses. MR goes to Europe for a vacation, but advises his secretary to make the required monthly payment to ME. MR's secretary uses the wrong mathematical formula to compute the interest and, therefore, pays a little less than is due. ME elects to accelerate and foreclose because of this minor default. MR returns from Europe, makes late tender of the unpaid interest and requests the court to set aside the acceleration. In many states, the courts will not grant relief for breach of contract resulting from MR's negligence. *See* Graf v. Hope Building Corp., 254 N.Y. 1, 171

N.E. 884 (1930). The trend, however, is to grant MR relief when acceleration is unconscionable under the circumstances. Although the willingness of MR to cure the default is not sufficient reason to grant equitable relief under this modern view, other factors such as MR's good faith and the unusual situation indicate that the acceleration should be set aside. *See* Campbell v. Werner, 232 So.2d 252 (Fla. App.1970); Federal Home Loan Mortgage Corp. v. Taylor, 318 So.2d 203 (Fla.App.1975).

F. Due-On-Sale Clauses

Mortgages often provide for acceleration if the mortgagor transfers any interest in the mortgaged property without the mortgagee's consent. These "due-on-sale" clauses present special legal problems that are discussed in an earlier chapter. *See* Ch. 6, pp. 105–111.

III. RIGHT TO POSSESSION AND RENTS

A. The Significance of Mortgage Theories

In Chapter 1 it is noted that the title, intermediate, and lien mortgage theories are significant today primarily as they relate to possession of the mortgaged property. Possession is important because with it comes the right to collect rents and profits.

A basic tenet of common law is that possession is an attribute of legal title. Thus, in title theory states the mortgagee receives the right to possession when the mortgage is executed. In intermediate theory jurisdictions the mortgagee ostensibly receives title, but is allowed by law to take possession only upon default. In lien theory states the mortgagee does not receive title and, therefore, cannot take possession at any time, even after default.

The confusion created by these conflicting theories has been somewhat alleviated by the almost universal practice of dealing with the issue of possession in the mortgage contract itself. The modern mortgage normally provides that the mortgagor has the right to possession until default and the mortgagee the right thereafter. *See* ¶ 20 of the Standard Mortgage in Appendix A. In a few lien theory states, however, mortgage agreements of this type are void as against public policy. But even in these jurisdictions, the mortgagor may give possession to the mortgagee after default.

Hence, as a practical matter, default gives the mortgagee the right to possession either by operation of law or by mortgage provision in all but a handful of jurisdictions. The consequences of this right are explored in the next section.

B. Mortgagee in Possession

1. Definition

When the mortgagee lawfully exercises dominion and control over the property under the mortgage, he is known as a mortgagee in possession. A mortgagee may become a mortgagee in posses-

[*143*]

sion without actually entering or occupying the mortgaged property so long as he exercises substantially the same control over the property as the mortgagor normally would exert.

> *Illustration*: MR executes a mortgage on a vacant farm to ME. The mortgage authorizes ME to take possession upon default. MR defaults. ME need not physically enter the farm to become a mortgagee in possession. Maintaining the property and seeking tenants would be sufficient.

2. Rights

A mortgagee in possession may control the property until either redemption or foreclosure occurs and collect all rents and profits arising from the land during that time. The mortgagee, of course, does not acquire title to the mortgaged property merely by taking possession of it under the mortgage.

3. Duties

All states impose trustee like duties on a mortgagee in possession.

a. Management

A mortgagee in possession must manage and maintain the property in a prudent manner and apply receipts in excess of costs to the mortgage debt. The duty of prudent management requires that a mortgagee in possession use reasonable efforts to make the property productive. He is, therefore, chargeable for rent he could have secured but for lack of reasonable diligence. And, if he merely occupies the property for his own use, he is generally accountable for the fair rental value of his occupancy without regard to whether the property produces more or less than that amount.

b. Accounting

A mortgagee in possession does not act free from judicial scrutiny. The mortgagor can require him to make a detailed accounting of receipts and expenses, but only in a foreclosure action or upon redemption.

c. Liability to Third Parties

A mortgagee in possession may incur liabilities to third parties. He is responsible in tort for his negligence in managing the mortgaged property and in contract for goods and services properly supplied to the property during his possession.

4. The Problem of Leases Existing at Default

When the mortgaged property is subject to a lease at the time of default, a mortgagee who has the right to take possession either by law or by agreement can ascertain his rights and duties vis-a-vis the lessee only by determining whether the lease was made before or after the execution of the mortgage. (It is presumed in the following discussion that all instruments were promptly recorded after execution so that the order of their execution is also the order of their priority under applicable recording statutes. *See* Ch. 9, pp. 158–159.)

a.   Prior Leases

If the lease was executed before the mortgage, the mortgagee in possession is bound by the lease because his security extends only to the interest the mortgagor owned at the time the mortgage was created. The lessee under a prior lease is also bound because the mortgagee in possession succeeds to the mortgagor's reversion and thereby establishes privity of estate. Hence, the lessee may remain on the property, but must pay rent to the mortgagee in possession.

b.   Junior Leases

If the lease was executed after the mortgage, the mortgagee may take possession and thereby terminate the lease on the theory that the lessee can have no greater right to possession than his lessor. Although the mortgagee appears to be in a generally favorable position in this situation, he is really at an advantage only if he desires to terminate the junior lease. If he wants to continue the junior lease and collect rent from the lessee, difficulty arises because the lessee is liable only to one with whom he is in either privity of contract or privity of estate. The junior lessee clearly has no contractual obligation to the mortgagee. In addition, no privity of estate exists between the junior lessee and the mortgagee because the mortgage could not transfer the mortgagor's reversion against a lessee not then in existence. The mortgagee, therefore, faces "Catch 22" of real estate finance law. Because he cannot force the junior lessee to enter a contract with him, he is entitled to receive rent only if he can establish privity of estate with the lessee. If, however, he attempts to do so by taking possession, the junior lease and the lessee's obligations thereunder are destroyed on the ground that the mortgagee's possession relates back to the date the mortgage was executed.

The mortgagee in possession may, of course, avoid this dilemma by persuading the junior lessee to enter an attornment agreement recognizing him as lessor. This arrangement establishes the privity of contract necessary for him to enforce the lease. The attornment agreement is in reality a new lease. Hence, the lessee and the mortgagee in possession may choose to set entirely new terms.

Although many junior lessees attorn to a mortgagee in possession, others take advantage of the situation to rid themselves of what they consider to be a losing lease. This is disastrous to the mortgagee who was depending upon their rents to pay the mortgage debt.

The mortgagee, therefore, should take steps to insure that he can preserve and enforce junior leases after default. Four options are available. First, he could subordinate the mortgage to junior leases so that they would be treated as prior leases and, therefore, survive his possession. *See* Ch. 9, pp. 161, 166. Second, he could require the mortgagor to insert an attornment provision in each valuable junior lease whereby the junior lessee agrees to recognize the mortgagee as landlord if the lessor/mortgagor defaults on the mortgage. The lessee, of course, may seek to have the mortgagee execute a non-disturbance agreement in return. Such a combination of attornment and non-disturbance agreements is the rough functional equivalent of a subordination. Third, the mortgagee could require that the mortgagor assign leases and rents as additional security for the underlying obligation. This alternative is explored in the following subsection. Fourth, at default the mortgagee could seek the appointment of a receiver of rents, a course of action that is discussed later in this chapter.

C. Assignment of Leases and Rents

In most jurisdictions the mortgagee may require the mortgagor to execute a conditional assignment of leases and rents giving him a lien on all present and future leases and rents independent of any right he may have to take possession of the mortgaged property. In a few lien theory states, an assignment of leases and rents made before default is void as against public policy.

The practical effect of a conditional assignment of leases and rents is that upon default the mortgagee, as assignee of the mortgagor's rights, may collect rents without taking possession under the mortgage. Thus, he can preserve and enforce junior leases until foreclosure.

In most states recognizing the assignment of leases and rents, the mortgagee may exercise his rights under the assignment by giving notice to the lessees to pay rent to him instead of the mortgagor. In some lien theory states, however, the mortgagee can activate the assignment only by commencing foreclosure proceedings and requesting the appointment of a receiver.

A conditional assignment of leases and rents also protects the mortgagee from being bound by agreements for advance rental payment, rent reduction, or lease cancellation commonly used by mortgagors in distress to "milk" the mortgaged property of all potential revenue. If the mortgagee obtains an assignment, records it and gives notice to existing lessees, all lessees enter advance payment, rent reduction, and cancellation agreements with the mortgagor at their peril.

D. Receiver

1. Background

In all jurisdictions the mortgagee may seek to have a receiver for rents and profits appointed in an action for foreclosure. This is a particularly valuable right in lien theory states where the mortgagee cannot obtain possession and reach rent and profits absent the mortgagor's agreement that he may do so.

Even when the mortgagee has the right to possession of the property upon default, he may prefer to have a receiver appointed rather than take possession himself. Three reasons support this preference. First, the stringent accounting duties imposed on a mortgagee in possession are avoided. Second, the potential tort and contract liability of a mortgagee in possession are eliminated. Third, junior leases are preserved and rents may be collected under those leases even when there is no assignment of leases and rents.

2. Grounds for Appointment

The receivership is an equitable remedy designed to preserve the mortgaged property pending foreclosure. The appointment of a receiver is generally within the sound discretion of the court bounded only by the traditional requirement that the court give due consideration to the financial position of the mortgagor, the adequacy of the security, and the danger of waste, destruction, or loss of the mortgaged property. Judicial authority in this area has been further broadened by the common use of a mortgage clause authorizing the mortgagee to obtain the appointment of a receiver. *See* ¶ 20 of the Standard Mortgage in Appendix A.

Courts have exercised their virtually unbridled discretion in markedly different ways. In many jurisdictions the appointment of a receiver is almost automatic upon request. In others a receiver is appointed only in the most compelling circumstances.

3. Receiver's Powers

Once appointed, the receiver is generally empowered to preserve the mortgagee's security by taking possession of the mortgaged property and collecting rents and profits. Although an exhaustive discussion of a receiver's specific powers is beyond the scope of these materials, three areas of receiver action deserve additional discussion.

a. Collecting Rent From Junior Lessees

A mortgagee may utilize a receiver to reach rent payable under a lease entered after the execution of the mortgage even when there is no assignment of leases and rents. The receiver's action is that of the court, not the mortgagee, so it does not automatically destroy the junior lease.

b. Collecting Rent From the Mortgagor in Possession

A vexing rent collection problem arises when the mortgagor occupies the mortgaged property as a residence or for other nonincome producing purposes. Although the general rule is that a receiver may collect occupational rent from the mortgagor, the New York courts prohibit a receiver from doing so if he was appointed under a clause in the mortgage rather than solely upon general equitable principles. *See* Holmes v. Gravenhorst, 263 N.Y. 148, 188 N.E. 285 (1933).

c. Operating the Mortgagor's Business

Mortgagees often request the appointment of a receiver to operate the mortgagor's business pending foreclosure. A court generally will grant the request only if the business is either specifically covered by the mortgage or based primarily on the rental value of the mortgaged property, as in the case of an apartment building.

IV. EQUITY OF REDEMPTION

A. Availability

Certain qualified individuals may prevent foreclosure by paying off the mortgage debt before the completion of foreclosure proceedings. This right of late payment is known as the equity of redemption. *See* Ch. 1, pp. 4–5.

B. Individuals Who May Redeem

The mortgagor, of course, may redeem. In addition, anyone acquiring an interest in or a lien on the mortgaged property after the attachment of the mortgage may redeem because their interests will be cut off by foreclosure. Eligible redemptioners include grantees, heirs, devisees, junior lessees, and junior encumbrancers. When several individuals have redemption rights, they may redeem in the order of the priority of their interests subject to the mortgagor's ultimate right to redeem.

C. Amount Required for Redemption

Equitable redemption generally can be accomplished only by paying the entire mortgage debt. However, in the event that the entire debt is not in default, as in the case of an unaccelerated amortized loan, the mortgagor may reinstate the loan and avoid foreclosure by making late payment of the overdue amount. (In the following discussion it is presumed that the entire mortgage debt is in default.)

D. Effect of Redemption

1. By the Mortgagor or His Successor

Redemption by the mortgagor or his successor discharges the mortgage lien. Junior interests survive unless also paid off.

2. By a Junior Interest Holder

Redemption by a junior interest holder does not terminate the mortgage from which the property is redeemed. On the contrary, the mortgage survives and the one who redeems is subrogated to the rights of the mortgagee. *See* Ch. 7, pp. 131–132.

> *Illustration*: MR executes a $10,000 first mortgage to ME–1, then a $5,000 second mortgage to ME–2 and finally a $2,000 third mortgage to ME–3. MR defaults on all loans and each mortgagee accelerates. MR may pay ME–1 $10,000 and free the land from the first mortgage. In that case, the second and third mortgage liens would remain. ME–2 also may pay ME–1 $10,000 before MR does so. This would not terminate the first mortgage. All three mortgages would remain, but now ME–2 would hold both the first and second mortgages. ME–3 could then redeem from ME–2 by paying him the total amount of the first and second liens ($15,000). This would not terminate either the first or second mortgages. All three mortgages would remain, but now would be held by ME–3. MR has the last right to redeem. He, however, must now pay ME–3 the total of all mortgage liens ($17,000) to redeem the land free from encumbrances.

E. Enforcement of the Right to Redeem

If the parties cannot agree on the question of redemption, the one asserting a right to redeem may file a bill in equity to enforce this right.

F. Waiver/Clogging

The courts will not recognize mortgage clauses purporting to waive or "clog" the mortgagor's equity of redemption. *See* Ch. 1, pp. 4–5.

G. When the Right of Redemption Ends

1. Foreclosure

The completion of foreclosure terminates the right of redemption of all parties defendant. If foreclosure is by judicial sale, the right to redeem generally ends when the court confirms the sale. If foreclosure is by power of sale, it ends when the sale is final under local law.

A junior interest holder omitted from the fore-closure proceedings retains both his interest and an equity of redemption. He, therefore, may seek to assert his right to redeem even after foreclosure. *See* Ch. 10, p. 186.

2. Termination by Other Means

A mortgagor's right to redeem may be barred by estoppel, laches, or a statute of limitations on the recovery of land. Generally none of these possibilities will arise if the mortgagor remains on the mortgaged property. It is only when the mortgagee takes possession that circumstances are ripe for the development of these bars to redemption.

V. ALTERNATIVES TO FORECLOSURE

Although a mortgagee generally is entitled to commence foreclosure proceedings immediately after default, he may decide to pursue another course of action.

A. Workout Arrangement

Institutional mortgage lenders desire to avoid foreclosure. Their business is to obtain a reasonable return on their investments, not to engage in litigation. Consequently, they often lower monthly payments, extend the time for payment, waive late charges, or make any other reasonable arrangement that allows the mortgagor to work his way out of temporary financial difficulty.

B. Deed in Lieu of Foreclosure

If the mortgagor cannot possibly pay the mortgage obligation, the mortgagee may be willing to accept a deed to the property in lieu of foreclosure. *See* Ch. 6, pp. 103–104.

C. Recovery on the Note Alone/"One Action" Rule

Even if litigation is necessary, the mortgagee generally may sue on the note without foreclosing the mortgage on the theory that because the underlying obligation is the principal element of the transaction, the mortgagee may treat it as unsecured if he so wishes. In California and a few other states, however, the mortgagee's only remedy on default is to foreclose and seek a deficiency judgment if appropriate. *See* Ch. 10, p. 187. This "one action" rule is based on the theory that because the mortgaged property is the primary fund for repayment of the debt, the mortgagee must exhaust it before attempting to reach the mortgagor's other assets. The rule is also designed to protect the mortgagor from multiple actions arising from the same loan transaction.

Where suit on the note alone is permitted, the mortgage is not affected by the resulting personal judgment against the mortgagor. The debt merges into the judgment and the judgment becomes the underlying obligation. Anything the mortgagee then collects from the mortgagor's other assets is credited against this obligation. The only significant change in the legal relationship of the parties is that enforcement of the underlying obligation is now governed by the statute of limitations on judgments rather than by the statute of limitations on promissory notes.

CHAPTER 9

PRIORITIES

I. GENERAL PRINCIPLES

When foreclosure is imminent, the mortgagee and other parties holding interests in the mortgaged property become particularly concerned about the priority of their respective interests. Their concern is well founded. First, interests acquired before the mortgage survive foreclosure; those acquired after the mortgage are extinguished. Second, the mortgagee and subsequent lienors are paid from the proceeds of the foreclosure sale in the order of their priority and the proceeds are usually insufficient to pay everyone.

II. RECORDING STATUTES

The principle "prior in time, prior in right" determines the order of priority among interest holders in the mortgaged property unless a subsequent purchaser fits within the protection afforded by the local recording statute. Recording statutes vary with regard to the requirements that a subsequent purchaser must meet. He must either (1) be without notice of the prior interest (notice statute), (2) be without notice of the prior interest and record first (race-notice statute) or (3) record first (race statute). In all jurisdictions the prior interest holder may preserve his original priority position by recording his interest immediately after its acquisition.

Illustration: MR executes a mortgage to ME–1 who records immediately. MR then executes a mortgage to ME–2. ME–2 cannot change the order of priority under any type of recording statute because he is on constructive notice of the prior interest and has also lost the race to record.

III. SELECTED PRIORITY PROBLEMS

Priority issues are inextricably entwined with the development of certain fundamental mortgage concepts. Thus, several priority problems are discussed in earlier chapters. *See* Chapter 4 (future advances and dragnet clauses), Chapter 5 (after-acquired property clauses), Chapter 6 (acquisition of the mortgaged property by the mortgagee), and Chapter 7 (conflicting and fractional assignments). Additional selected priority matters are presented here. In this discussion it is presumed, unless otherwise indicated, that all mortgages and other interests were recorded immediately after their acquisition.

A. The Purchase Money Mortgage

1. *Distinguishing Features*

The purchase money mortgage is a mortgage taken by the seller of real estate as security for part of the purchase price or by a third party lender as security for purchase funds advanced.

See Ch. 3, pp. 41–42. In either situation, purchase money mortgage status is available only when the deed and mortgage are part of one continuous transaction.

> *Illustration*: MR desires to purchase certain land for sale in another part of the state. He does not have sufficient cash on hand to do so. Thus, he asks ME to loan him $20,000. ME advances MR $20,000 to purchase the land. MR gives ME a $20,000 promissory note and agrees to secure the note with a mortgage on the property when he acquires it. Later that day MR travels to the land and makes an offer to purchase it. After three days of protracted negotiations, the transaction is completed and MR receives a deed to the property. MR returns home and on the second day following his return executes a mortgage on the property to ME. This is a purchase money mortgage. As long as the mortgage is an inseparable aspect of the acquisition of the mortgaged property, it need not be executed at the same time as the deed. *See* Stewart v. Smith, 36 Minn. 82, 30 N.W. 430 (1836).

2. *Preferred Priority Position*

A purchase money mortgage has priority over any interest attaching to the property through the purchaser-mortgagor. Underlying this principle is the equitable theory that when the mortgagor receives the property, it is already encumbered with a lien in favor of the purchase money mortgagee whose willingness to extend credit or advance funds made the acquisition possible. Accordingly, a purchase money mortgage takes precedence over judgment liens against the mortgagor, liens arising from after-acquired property clauses in other mortgages executed by the mortgagor, and claims against the mortgagor for dower and homestead.

> *Illustration*: JL obtains a judgment against MR and receives a judgment lien on all real estate owned by MR. Later MR borrows money from ME to purchase a parcel of land. MR executes a mortgage on the land to ME to secure repayment of the loan. Under the purchase money mortgage rule, ME's mortgage lien has priority over JL's judgment lien.

The priority of a lien or other interest existing on the property at the time of its acquisition by the mortgagor is not affected by the purchase money mortgage rule. The rule only postpones liens and claims that attach to the property through the mortgagor.

> *Illustration*: O owns a parcel of land. JL obtains a judgment against O and receives a judgment lien on all real estate owned by O including the land in question. The lien is of record. O then conveys the land to MR. The lien is not discharged. MR pays O with funds borrowed from ME and executes a mortgage on the land to ME to secure repayment of the loan. Although ME's mortgage qualifies as a purchase money mortgage, it does not take precedence over JL's prior lien on the property.

B. Subordination Agreements

Established priorities may be altered by agreement. Such an agreement is called a subordination because it involves a senior interest holder voluntarily subordinating his rights to those of a junior interest holder. Three common subordination situations are treated in this subsection.

1. *Subordination of a Purchase Money Mortgage to a Construction Loan Mortgage*

a. Background

Subordination agreements are often employed as part of the real estate development process. Developers, of course, need raw land upon which to construct shopping centers, apartment houses, office buildings, subdivisions and other projects. Because developers are typically unable to purchase land outright and because institutional lenders are generally reluctant to make land acquisition loans, sellers often finance the sale themselves. This form of financing is not difficult to implement. The seller conveys the land to the developer in exchange for a small down payment and a note for the balance of the purchase price secured by a purchase money mortgage on the land conveyed. The developer then obtains financing for the actual development. Construction lenders, however, normally demand a first lien on the property as security. In order for the planned development to occur, the seller, therefore, must subordinate his purchase money mortgage to the construction loan mortgage. He is usually willing to take this risk on the expectation that the development will enhance the prop-

erty's value to the extent that he will be in a
better security position as a second mortgagee of
improved land than as a first mortgagee of unimproved land. Moreover, he typically is able to
demand a higher than normal purchase price for
the property as compensation for agreeing to the
subordination.

b. The Subordination Agreement in General

The subordination is normally part of the original agreement between the seller and the developer and is covered in either the real estate
contract, the purchase money mortgage, or a
separate document. An advance subordination
agreement may take either of two forms: (1) an
agreement that subordination occurs automatically when the construction loan mortgage is executed or (2) an agreement to execute a formal subordination upon request once the construction loan
is obtained.

c. Describing the Construction Loan

The subordination agreement must contain an
adequate description of the construction loan. If
it does not, the courts refuse to enforce the
agreement on the ground it is impossible to tell
what has been promised.

The question of whether the description of the
construction loan is so indefinite as to render the
subordination contract unenforceable is often dif-

ficult to resolve. Although the courts generally agree that the maximum amount of the construction loan must be stated, they disagree as to whether the interest rate, maturity, or other loan details must also be specified. Furthermore, in some states a less detailed subordination agreement is permitted when the missing terms are left for determination to an institutional construction lender. This approach is based on the rationale that institutional lenders are bound by regulation, custom, and usage to impose reasonable loan terms.

In California the indefinite description issue is further complicated by a decision of the Supreme Court of that state requiring all subordination agreements to be just and reasonable to the seller. Handy v. Gordon, 65 Cal.2d 578, 55 Cal. Rptr. 769, 422 P.2d 329 (1967). What this "fairness" doctrine demands with regard to precision in describing the construction loan remains an open question.

d. Obtaining the Construction Loan Described

If the developer obtains a construction loan that varies materially from the loan described in the subordination agreement, subordination does not occur.

e. Diversion of Construction Loan Funds

Priority problems may arise even after the specified construction loan is obtained. Occasionally a mortgagor-developer diverts loan proceeds from the project with the result that the property is not sufficiently enhanced in value to adequately secure the subordinated purchase money mortgage loan. In such case, the purchase money mortgagee is likely to claim that the subordination agreement has been breached and his original lien priority restored. When this issue first arose, the courts generally held that, in the absence of an agreement to the contrary, a construction loan mortgagee acting in good faith has no duty to monitor the application of construction funds. The construction lender, therefore, retained the lien priority granted to him in the subordination agreement unless he advanced money to the developer in bad faith.

This principle survives, but its significance has been eroded by two developments. First, purchase money mortgagees commonly condition subordination upon actual use of the construction loan funds for construction purposes. Second, a similar condition may be implied in certain cases. *See* Middlebrook-Anderson Co. v. Southwest Sav. & Loan Ass'n, 18 Cal.App.3d 1023, 96 Cal.Rptr. 338 (1971).

When subordination is expressly or impliedly conditioned in this fashion and funds are diverted, the purchase money mortgagee is clearly entitled to relief. The purchase money mortgage is generally restored to priority over the construction loan mortgage to the extent of the diverted funds. Thus, lien priority is as follows: (1) construction lender for funds properly applied to the project, (2) purchase money mortgagee for the full amount of his mortgage, and (3) construction lender for diverted funds.

f.   The Optional Advance Risk

Even if all funds are used for construction, the construction lender may lose priority to the subordinated purchase money mortgage for advances made ahead of schedule or after default on the theory such advances are optional, not obligatory. *See* Ch. 4, pp. 69–70.

2.   *Subordination of a Lease to a Mortgage and Vice Versa*

A mortgagee may desire to enhance his security position by switching priorities with a lessee of the mortgaged property. Reversal of priorities may occur in either direction. If an unattractive lease has original priority, the mortgagee might demand subordination of the lease to the mortgage as a condition of making the mortgage loan. The subordination enables the mortgagee to terminate the lease if he takes possession after default or forecloses. If an attractive lease is originally junior to the mortgage, the mortgage might subordinate the mortgage to the lease in order to collect rents from the lessee on default and preserve the lease at foreclosure. *See* Ch. 8, pp. 146–148.

3. Subordination of the Fee to a Leasehold Mortgage

Leasehold mortgagees frequently require the *Zaiger* owner of the leased property to submit his fee interest to the mortgage lien. Although this arrangement is commonly termed subordination of the fee, it obviously does not involve switching lien priorities. *See* Ch. 3, pp. 56–58.

C. Fixtures

The mortgage is a lien on all fixtures on the mortgaged property. *See* Ch. 5, pp. 89–90. These fixtures may also be subject to the lien of a security interest that attached to them before they became fixtures. Controversy often arises between the mortgagee and the holder of the security interest regarding the priority of their respective liens.

Section 9–313 of the 1962 Official Text of the Uniform Commercial Code ("U.C.C.") was designed to resolve this priority issue. Unfortunately, it did not. Although all states but Louisiana adopted the U.C.C., a great number of them substantially amended or omitted Section 9–313.

Because the original Section 9–313 received lukewarm acceptance, the National Conference of

Commissioners on Uniform State Laws proposed a revised version of that section in 1972. The legislatures of several states have enacted the 1972 Official Text revision.

Today the states can be divided into three categories with regard to the fixture priority issue: (1) those following the 1962 U.C.C. Official Text, (2) those following the 1972 U.C.C. Official Text and (3) those with their own variations. Detailed analysis of any of these approaches is beyond the scope of this book. Nonetheless, a few general comments about the two U.C.C. versions are appropriate here.

1. The 1962 U.C.C.

The 1962 U.C.C. Official Text generally preferred the holder of a purchase money security interest in the fixture over the mortgagee. Under the original Section 9–313, a fixture financer gained priority over existing mortgages by the attachment of his security interest before installation, no filing was required. He could also achieve priority over subsequent mortgages and subsequent advances made under an existing construction loan mortgage by filing first, even if the financing statement was filed against a contractor and, thus, was not in the chain of title of the mortgaged property.

2. *The 1972 U.C.C.*

Severe criticism of these elements of the original Section 9–313 led to the 1972 revision. The 1972 Official Text eliminates the concept of priority by the attachment alone. As between the holder of a security interest in fixtures and the mortgagee, the first to file takes priority. A purchase money security interest filed before or within ten days after the goods become fixtures, however, still takes priority over existing nonconstruction loan mortgages on the theory that the party who supplies the money used to acquire the fixtures should be favored. But, because a construction lender provides funds for the entire improvement and expects all parts thereof to serve as collateral for his loan, existing construction loan mortgages now take complete priority over purchase money security interests in goods that become fixtures during construction. Finally, with regard to the chain of title problem, the 1972 Code requires that fixture financing statements be filed in real estate records where they can be located by a real estate title search.

D. Mechanics' Lien Statutes

1. *General*

Mechanics' lien statutes exist in every state to give individuals who supply labor or materials to a construction project a lien on the property as security for payment due them. These statutes vary greatly from state to state with regard to persons protected, the lien amount, lien priority, and numerous other factors.   Only general priority and constitutional issues are treated here.

2. *Priority*

Priority problems frequently arise between mechanics' lienors and mortgagees, particularly construction mortgage lenders.   Although all mechanics' lien statutes give the mechanics' lienor a priority preference, the nature of the preference is not uniform throughout the country.

a.   Relation Back Approach

In many states mechanics' lienor's priority relates back to the date construction began.   Under this relation back approach the construction lender can protect his lien against all mechanics' lienors merely by recording the construction loan mortgage before construction commences.   But, if he fails to do so, he loses priority to all mechanics' lienors, not just those who did work before the mortgage was recorded.

Illustration: MR decides to construct a building on his property, so he hires A to clear the land and excavate a cellar.   MR pays A.   Six weeks later, MR obtains a construction mortgage loan from ME who promptly records the mortgage.   After the mortgage is recorded, B does work on the building.   B is not paid.   He, therefore, files a mechanics' lien.   It relates back to the date A did the initial construction work and thereby takes priority over ME's mortgage.

Even when the construction loan mortgage is recorded before work begins, controversy may develop in relation back states as to the priority of future advances made by a construction lender over an intervening mechanics' lien. The issue usually arises when a mechanics' lienor contends that all construction advances made after the attachment of his lien are optional, not obligatory and thereby lose priority to his encumbrance. *See* Ch. 4, pp. 69–70.

b. Improvements v. Land Approach

In a number of states, mechanics' liens receive absolute priority on the improvements but not the land. In these jurisdictions a mechanics' lien on the improvement is even superior to a construction loan mortgage recorded before construction commenced.

Illustration: MR executes a construction loan mortgage to ME who records. The unimproved land is worth $20,000. Construction commences two days after ME records. The completed building causes the parcel to increase in value to $100,000. ME has a first lien on the $20,000 attributable to the land. Any mechanics' liens that may arise have priority over ME as to the $80,000 attributable to the building.

c. Miscellaneous Approaches

The remaining states take a wide variety of approaches to the mechanics' lien priority issue.

A few give the mechanic priority from the date he actually began work. One or two date his lien from the time the basic construction contract was entered. Still others base priority on some other factor.

3. Constitutionality of Mechanics' Lien Statutes

Mechanics' lien statutes generally authorize mechanics and materialmen to perfect their liens without judicial involvement and sometimes without prior notice to the property owner. This procedure has been attacked in several jurisdictions as a denial of the property owner's Fourteenth Amendment due process rights.

Most courts faced with this issue have upheld the mechanics' lien statute in question on the theory that a mechanics' lien does not constitute a taking of property within the meaning of the Fourteenth Amendment. These courts reason that the attachment of the lien does not deprive the owner of possession, use, or enjoyment of his land and any impairment of his ability to sell or encumber the property is a de minimus taking that does not trigger the application of due process safeguards. A few courts, however, have concluded that a mechanics' lien affects a Fourteenth Amendment property interest by impairing the property owner's ability to alienate his land and also by reducing the value of his equity. These courts have further held that the standard

[172]

statutory procedures for perfecting a mechanics' lien are constitutionally defective and that property owners are entitled to notice of the lien and an early opportunity to be heard regarding its validity.

4. *Other Protection for Mechanics and Materialmen*

It is noted earlier in this section that in most states a prudent construction lender may secure priority over a mechanics' lienor by recording his construction loan mortgage before construction commences. Hence, if the project fails and the mortgagee forecloses, mechanics' lienors usually receive nothing from the foreclosure sale. To correct this inequity, some states have given mechanics and materialmen lien rights in addition to those they receive under the traditional mechanics' lien statute.

a. Stop Notice Statutes

In a few jurisdictions individuals who supply labor or materials to a construction project may obtain a statutory lien on construction loan money not yet disbursed by the lender. Legislation of this type is known as a stop notice statute. Under such a statute an unpaid mechanic or materialman may file a notice of claim with the lender who then must stop advancing funds for construction or at least withhold funds to cover the claim.

b.   Equitable Liens

Courts in several states have used the equitable lien concept to fashion a remedy for mechanics and materialmen similar to that available under stop notice statutes. Under the equitable lien approach an unpaid lien claimant may reach undisbursed construction loan funds if he can show special equities or establish that the lender has been unjustly enriched.

E.   Tax Liens

1.   *State and Local Property Tax Liens*

Statutes in most states impose a lien on real estate to secure the payment of taxes or assessments levied on the property. Usually these property tax and assessment liens are allowed to "leapfrog" existing encumbrances to the first lien priority position. In order to minimize the risk of losing priority to subsequent tax liens, mortgagees generally require the mortgagor to escrow funds for the payment of property taxes. *See* Ch. 4, p. 83.

2.   *Federal Income Tax Liens*

The federal government may obtain a lien against the real property of a delinquent income taxpayer. The federal tax lien arises upon assessment, but, unlike state property tax liens, does not receive priority over existing encumbrances. It is also not valid against subsequent

[*174*]

mortgages until notice of its existence is filed in the public records.

F. Lis Pendens

Under the common law doctrine of lis pendens the pendency of a suit concerning title to or possession of land imparts constructive notice to the world of the claims of the litigants. One who acquires an interest in property involved in litigation, therefore, takes subject to the judgment of the court. Because it is difficult to discover the existence of pending litigation, statutes in most states limit the application of the lis pendens doctrine by requiring that a seperate notice of the suit be filed.

Illustration: O conveys land to GE who records. O initiates suit to have the deed set aside and records a lis pendens notice as required by state law. GE executes a mortgage on the land to ME. The court then renders judgment in favor of O and sets aside the deed. Because ME was on lis pendens notice of O's interest, O takes the property free from ME's mortgage. In those states that continue to follow the common law lis pendens doctrine, O would take free from the mortgage even if he had failed to file separate notice of the suit.

G. Marshalling

The equitable doctrine of marshalling assets does not deal so much with determining the priority of interests in the mortgaged property as with equitably preserving the value of each interest

[*175*]

once priority has been established. The doctrine has two main facets: the two funds rule and the sale in inverse order of alienation rule.

1. Two Funds Rule

The two funds rule is the most familiar principle of marshalling. It provides that when a senior mortgagee has a claim against two funds and a junior mortgagee has a claim against only one, the senior mortgagee must enforce his claim so as to best preserve the value of the junior mortgagee's security. Although the senior mortgagee may proceed at law against either or both funds, equity requires him to seek satisfaction first from the fund the junior mortgagee cannot reach. Only when this fund is exhausted may the senior mortgagee proceed against the sole fund to which the junior mortgagee has access.

Illustration: MR owns two parcels of land, lot A worth $10,000 and lot B worth $4,000. MR borrows $12,000 from ME–1 and gives ME–1 a first mortgage on both lots. MR then borrows $5,000 from ME–2 and gives ME–2 a second mortgage on lot A. MR defaults on both mortgages. ME–1 forecloses on lot A only and the foreclosure sale brings $10,000. ME–1 claims the entire amount as first lienor. Although his $12,000 mortgage was a first lien on lot A, under the two funds rule he receives foreclosure sale proceeds as if he had satisfied himself first out of lot B and then out of lot A. Under this principle, ME–1 receives $8,000 (the amount of his lien minus the value of lot B) and ME–2 is entitled to $2,000.

Illustration: Assume the same fact situation as in the immediately preceding illustration except that no default occurs and ME–1 releases his lien on lot B. Under the two funds rule, ME–1 retains a first lien on lot A for only $8,000 (the amount of the original lien minus the value of lot B) and ME–2 has a second lien for $5,000.

2. Sale in Inverse Order of Alienation Rule

The doctrine of marshalling also applies when a large tract of mortgaged land is subdivided and sold in separate parcels to individuals who pay the full purchase price for their lots without obtaining a partial release of the blanket mortgage. If the blanket mortgage was recorded, its lien follows each lot into the hands of the lot purchaser. (Payment of the full purchase price to the mortgagor does not discharge the mortgagee's lien.) Although the purchaser would not have consummated the deal if he had searched the title, he is not completely unprotected. Equity gives him the right to require that the land retained by the seller be sold at foreclosure before his lot is sold. Because this concept favors the purchasers in the order they acquired lots, it is called the sale in inverse order of alienation rule.

Illustration: MR owns a 50 acre tract subject to a recorded mortgage in favor of ME. MR subdivides the tract into 50 one-acre lots and sells lots successively to A, B, and C who each pay the full purchase price for their respective lots. MR defaults on the blanket mortgage and ME forecloses. Under the sale in inverse order of alienation rule, equity requires the court to direct the sheriff to sell first the land retained by MR, then C's lot, then B's lot, and finally A's lot. The sale process ends whenever the cumulative proceeds are sufficient to satisfy the mortgage debt.

The sale in inverse order of alienation rule is of waning importance for several reasons. First, the rule is inapplicable when a purchaser pays a reduced purchase price for taking the property subject to the mortgage. Second, most purchasers making full payment search the record and demand a partial release of the mortgage. Third, the mortgagee may avoid application of the rule simply by placing an anti-marshalling clause in the mortgage.

3. Anti-Marshalling Agreement

Marshalling in either of its forms cannot be applied in the face of a contrary agreement. Mortgagees, therefore, often insist on a mortgage provision giving them the right to release or foreclose and sell parcels of the mortgaged property free from any requirement to marshall assets.

CHAPTER 10

FORECLOSURE

The evolution of the foreclosure concept is traced in Chapter 1. This chapter is designed to promote your understanding of the procedure as it presently exists.

I. AVAILABILITY AND PURPOSE OF FORECLOSURE

On default the mortgagee may have the mortgaged property sold to satisfy the unpaid mortgage debt. Although this process is customarily referred to as mortgage foreclosure, it is really the mortgagor's equity of redemption that is foreclosed.

The foreclosure process generally may be commenced by the mortgagee anytime after default. Its purpose is to cut off the mortgagor's equity of redemption and the rights of all persons who acquired interests in the land after the execution of the mortgage so that the person who purchases the property at foreclosure receives title as it existed immediately before the attachment of the mortgage. An important corollary of this principle is that interests acquired by third parties prior to the execution of the mortgage survive foreclosure. In this way the mortgagee obtains the full benefit of the security for which he bargained, but no more.

II. STATUTE OF LIMITATIONS

In most states the mortgagee must foreclose within a certain statutory period after maturity of the mortgage. Because needless controversy arises when the statute of limitations on the mortgage and the underlying debt differ (*See* Ch. 4, p. 86), the statutory trend is toward barring both simultaneously.

III. FORECLOSURE BY JUDICIAL SALE

Foreclosure by judicially approved sale is the principal method of foreclosure in this country. *See* Ch. 1, pp. 6–7. It is available in all states and the required method of foreclosure in many jurisdictions. Although court supervised foreclosure is the best way to determine the rights of the parties involved and thereby to produce the most marketable title, it is a complex, lengthy, and expensive procedure. The numerous legal difficulties inherent in this process are analyzed in this section.

A. Parties Defendant

A foreclosure decree affects only those persons before the court. The naming of parties defendant, therefore, is a critical step in the foreclosure process.

1. Necessary/Proper Parties

Parties defendant can be placed into two general categories: necessary parties and proper parties. A necessary party defendant to a foreclosure suit is anyone who must be joined in order to accomplish the purpose of foreclosure which, as previously noted, is to sell the mortgagor's interest in the property as it existed immediately before the execution of the mortgage. Thus, the mortgagor and all persons who acquired interests in the property after the execution of the mortgage are necessary parties and may be joined without their consent. The interests of necessary parties omitted from the suit survive foreclosure.

Illustration: MR executes a first mortgage to ME–1. MR then executes a second mortgage to ME–2, leases a part of the mortgage property to L and grants an easement over another part to X. MR defaults on the first mortgage and ME–1 commences foreclosure proceedings. MR, ME–2, L and X are all necessary parties defendant because their interests must be extinguished if the foreclosure sale purchaser is to receive MR's interest as it existed immediately before the first mortgage was executed.

A proper party defendant to a foreclosure suit is one whose joinder is desirable, but not essential to accomplish the purpose of foreclosure. Senior mortgagees and those who hold no interest in the property but are personally liable on the debt are proper parties. Although a person personally liable on the debt can be involuntarily joined, a senior mortgagee generally cannot be joined without his consent.

2. Mortgagor in Bankruptcy

The defendant mortgagor's bankruptcy may significantly alter the mortgagee's right to foreclose. The Bankruptcy Reform Act of 1978 provides that in all forms of bankruptcy the filing of a petition automatically stays the commencement or continuation of foreclosure proceedings against the debtor. 11 U.S.C.A. § 362. The Department of Housing and Urban Development, however, receives a limited exception from this automatic stay rule. It may still foreclose its mortgages that are federally insured and cover property consisting of five or more living units.

3. Mortgagor in Military Service

The Soldiers' and Sailors' Civil Relief Act of 1940, 50 U.S.C.App. § 510 *et seq.*, grants special protection to defendant mortgagors on active duty in the armed forces. The Act provides that a serviceperson may apply to a court to set aside default judgments rendered against him on either pre-service or in-service obligations. The mortgagee, therefore, must file an affidavit specifying the military status of a mortgagor who does not answer the foreclosure complaint. Failure to file an affidavit does not affect the validity of the proceedings against a civilian defendant who does not appear. If, however, the mortgagor is in the

armed forces, the foreclosure can be properly
completed only if the serviceperson appears or is
represented at the proceedings.

Once the serviceperson has appeared or is represented before the court, he may seek additional
relief under the stay provisions of the Act. His
ability to stay the foreclosure proceedings depends primarily on whether the mortgage obligation was incurred before or after his entry on
active duty. If the mortgage is a pre-service
obligation and the mortgagor's ability to meet the
debt has been materially affected by military
service, the court must stay the foreclosure or
grant other appropriate equitable relief. If the
mortgage is an in-service obligation, the court
may stay the foreclosure only if the mortgagor's
ability to participate in the foreclosure proceedings is materially affected by his military service.

4. *Intentional Omission of Junior Lessees*

When a junior lease is particularly favorable to
the lessor, it is to the mortgagee's advantage to
keep the lease alive through foreclosure and
thereby enhance the sale value of his security.
Because the rights of a junior interest holder not
made a party defendant survive foreclosure, it
would appear that a mortgagee could preserve a
valuable junior lease merely by omitting the lessee from the foreclosure suit. In some states the
mortgagee may keep a junior lease alive in this
fashion. In other jurisdictions, however, foreclo-

sure extinguishes an intentionally omitted junior lease, at least when the lessee does not want to preserve it. This approach may be justified on the ground that joinder requirements are for the protection of junior interest holders, not the mortgagee.

In view of the uncertainty that exists with regard to preserving intentionally omitted junior leases, the mortgagees sometimes subordinate the mortgage to a valuable junior lease to insure that the lease will survive foreclosure. *See* Ch. 9, pp. 161, 166.

5. *Lis Pendens*

Under the doctrine of lis pendens, parties who acquire an interest in the mortgaged property with notice of the foreclosure proceedings are bound by the foreclosure decree just as if they had been named parties defendant. *See* Ch. 9, p. 175.

B. Judicial Sale Procedures

The judicial foreclosure sale procedure is governed by statutory law that varies from state to state. These statutes normally call for a public sale conducted by the sheriff or a court appointed official.

C. Confirmation/Adequacy of the Sale Price

Foreclosure by judicial sale is incomplete until it is confirmed by the court. Absent fraud or chilled bidding, the inadequacy of the foreclosure sale price is generally not a ground upon which a court will refuse to confirm. Statutes in some states require that the purchase price must be a certain percentage of the appraised value of the property, but mortgagors generally waive appraisal as a matter of course.

D. The Purchaser

1. Purchaser's Title

The purchaser at a judicial foreclosure sale receives title to the property as it existed in the hands of the mortgagor immediately before the execution of the mortgage being foreclosed. Although the rights of the mortgagor, the mortgagee, and junior interest holders named parties defendant are extinguished, the rights of individuals who acquired interests prior to the execution of the mortgage survive foreclosure.

Illustration: MR grants an easement over his property to X. MR then executes a first mortgage to ME–1, a second mortgage to ME–2, a third mortgage to ME–3 and a lease of part of the property to L. ME–2 properly forecloses and P acquires title at the sale. Although the interests of MR, ME–2, ME–3 and L end at foreclosure, P takes the property subject to the interests of X and ME–1.

The sale proceeds are used to pay the mortgage debt. Consequently, the purchaser is also subrogated to the rights of the mortgagee. *See* Ch. 7, p. 133. This concept is important in determining the purchaser's position vis-a-vis a junior lienor omitted from the original foreclosure proceeding.

2. *Purchaser Versus Omitted Junior Lienor*

When a junior lienor is not named as a party defendant, his lien survives foreclosure. Thus, he may still either foreclose his lien or redeem the senior mortgage. *See* Ch. 8, pp. 152–155. The purchaser at the foreclosure sale, however, may eliminate the omitted junior lien by using any one of three methods: redemption, reforeclosure, or strict foreclosure.

Because the purchaser succeeds to the mortgagor's right to redeem junior liens, he may extinguish the omitted junior lien by simply paying it off. The purchaser is also subrogated to the mortgagee's right to foreclose. He, therefore, may eliminate the omitted lien by reforeclosing the mortgage or in some states by strictly foreclosing the rights of the junior lienor.

3. *Purchase by the Mortgagee*

The mortgagee may purchase the mortgaged property at the foreclosure sale. Because he is entitled to receive as much of the sale proceeds as is necessary to satisfy the mortgage debt, he may bid up to that amount without having to produce any cash. As a consequence he often is the highest bidder at the sale.

4. *Purchase by the Mortgagor*

If the mortgagor or his agent purchases at the foreclosure sale, unpaid junior liens survive on the theory that the purchase was really payment of the senior lien. This is, of course, an exception to the rule that all properly joined junior interests are cut off by foreclosure.

E. Disbursement of the Sale Proceeds

The proceeds of the foreclosure sale are applied in the following order: (1) expenses of the foreclosure, (2) satisfaction of the mortgage debt, and (3) satisfaction of junior liens in the order of their priority. Any excess goes to the mortgagor.

F. Deficiency Judgment

1. *General*

If the foreclosure sale proceeds are insufficient to satisfy the underlying debt, the mortgagee may obtain a deficiency judgment against the mortgagor and anyone else personally liable on the debt.

Illustration: MR executes a $10,000 note and mortgage to ME. MR conveys the property to GE who assumes and agrees to pay the mortgage debt. GE defaults and ME forecloses. The foreclosure sale produces $8,000 after expenses. ME receives the $8,000 and may obtain a deficiency judgment for $2,000 against each MR and GE. Naturally, ME may recover no more than $2,000 on these judgments.

2. *Anti-Deficiency Legislation*

Depression era legislation still limits the recovery of deficiency judgments in several states. One statutory approach is to prohibit deficiency judgments in certain situations, such as in the case of purchase money mortgages or where foreclosure is by power of sale. Another approach is to limit deficiency judgments to the amount by which the debt exceeds the fair market value of the property. Waiver of the benefit of either type of anti-deficiency legislation is generally considered ineffective as against public policy.

IV. FORECLOSURE BY POWER OF SALE

Foreclosure by out-of-court sale is permitted in several states. This method of foreclosure is usually termed foreclosure by power of sale because it is based on a mortgage provision authorizing sale of the property without court supervision. Although foreclosure by power of sale represents a relatively expedient and inexpensive means of foreclosure, it is prohibited in many jurisdictions and where permitted, it is merely an alternative to foreclosure by judicial sale.

A. Comparison to Judicial Sale

Foreclosure by power of sale serves generally the same purpose as foreclosure by judicial sale. However, some significant differences exist.

1. Form of Security Device

Because the deed of trust is designed to be enforced by an out-of-court sale conducted by the trustee, it is a popular financing device in states where foreclosure by power of sale is permitted. A regular mortgage, of course, may be drafted to include a power of sale provision.

2. Sale Procedures

The procedure for foreclosure by power of sale is generally regulated by statute. These statutes usually provide for a public sale conducted only after proper notice. Typically notice by advertisement in a local newspaper for a prescribed period is required. In some states, additional notice by mail or personal service must be given to the mortgagor. Junior interest holders of record are entitled to such added notice in only a few of these jurisdictions.

3. Purchaser's Title

The purchaser at a power of sale foreclosure receives the same rights as a purchaser at a judicial foreclosure. Nonetheless, his title is generally less secure because the sale has not been confirmed by a court and is, therefore, more likely to be the subject of future litigation.

4. Purchase by the Lender

The form of the financing device authorizing foreclosure by power of sale determines whether the lender may bid at the sale. If a mortgage with a power of sale provision is involved, the mortgagee has a duty to conduct the sale in an impartial manner. Thus, he may not purchase the property unless he has contractual or statutory permission to do so. If a deed of trust is used, the lender may freely bid because the trustee conducts the sale.

5. *Deficiency or Surplus*

Foreclosure by power of sale is extrajudicial. Consequently, the mortgagee must take additional action when either a deficiency or surplus results. If the proceeds are insufficient to satisfy the mortgage debt, the mortgagee must bring a separate action to recover a deficiency judgment against a party personally liable on the underlying obligation. If the proceeds exceed the amount of the mortgage debt, the mortgagee must file an interpleader action to protect himself against liability for paying the surplus to the wrong parties.

6. *Judicial Review*

Although the courts do not oversee foreclosure by power of sale, the process is always subject to later judicial scrutiny. This possibility reduces the value of the property to prospective purchasers and may cause the mortgagee to forego foreclosure by power of sale in favor of foreclosure by judicial sale.

B. Constitutional Issues

Foreclosure by power of sale is currently under constitutional attack. Some authorities argue that the notice and hearing procedures used in the typical power of sale foreclosure do not meet the due process requirements of the Fifth and Fourteenth Amendments. This attack really involves several issues.

1. *Governmental Action*

The Fifth and Fourteenth Amendments limit governmental action, not private activity. The first issue, therefore, is whether a power of sale foreclosure involves significant federal or state action.

The federal action question usually arises when the foreclosure mortgage is either an instrumentality of the federal government such as the Veterans Administration or a private entity closely related to the federal government such as the Federal National Mortgage Association. The few courts that have considered the question have tended to find federal action if the mortgagee is a member of the former category, but not if he is a member of the latter. The problem with this approach is that it is difficult to fit some hybrid organizations such as the Federal Home Loan Mortgage Corporation and the Government National Mortgage Association into either category. Thus, the federal action question remains partly unresolved.

The state action question is relatively well settled. The prevailing view is that power of sale foreclosure does not involve state action. Courts generally conclude that this method of foreclosure is established by private contract even though it may be recognized and regulated by state statute. Unsuccessful arguments for state action have been based on encouragement, enforcement, and participation theories.

2. *Notice and Hearing*

In those instances in which foreclosure by power of sale is considered to involve governmental action, due process requires that the mortgagor and other interested parties receive adequate notice of the foreclosure and a presale opportunity to be heard. In order to determine whether these requirements have been met, it is necessary to examine the mortgage documents in question and the applicable local statutes. Such an examination reveals that traditional power of sale procedures rarely satisfy due process standards. The notice given often is not reasonably calculated to reach all interested parties. Moreover, a presale hearing is not normally held.

3. *Waiver*

Even assuming that the requisite governmental action is present and that the local procedure violates either the Fifth Amendment or the Fourteenth Amendment, the traditional power of sale procedure may still be followed if the mortgagor knowingly and voluntarily waives his procedural due process rights. The validity of individual waivers, of course, can only be determined on a case by case basis.

V. STRICT FORECLOSURE

Strict foreclosure was the method originally used to extinguish the mortgagor's equity of redemption. A defaulting mortgagor was given a set period of time to pay the debt or forever lose his interest in the mortgaged property. This means of foreclosure was not generally accepted in this country. *See* Ch. 1, pp. 5–6. Today, strict foreclosure is available as a principal method of foreclosure in only three states. In several other jurisdictions, however, its use is authorized against necessary parties omitted from a prior judicial foreclosure suit.

Statutes in a few New England states provide for a special form of strict foreclosure that is accomplished by entry plus possession for a specific time period, often three years. The effect is the same as the traditional form of strict foreclosure. The mortgagor's equity of redemption is extinguished without sale.

VI. STATUTORY REDEMPTION

A. Availability

Although the equitable right of redemption ends at foreclosure, statutes in approximately one-half of the states establish a right to redeem the mortgaged property *after* the foreclosure sale. The purpose of statutory redemption is to protect the mortgagor and junior interest holders from sale of the property at a price far below its value. Statutory redemption laws vary considerably, but all specify a certain time period, often one year, within which redemption must be accomplished. *See* Ch. 1, p. 7.

As a general rule, the mortgagor may retain possession of the mortgaged property during the statutory redemption period. If redemption is not accomplished by the end of that period, the purchaser at the foreclosure sale receives title to and possession of the property.

B. Individuals Who May Redeem

The mortgagor, his successors, and any junior lienor joined in the foreclosure may exercise a right of redemption under most statutes. The mortgagor and his successors generally are given an exclusive right to redeem for a specified period of time. After the mortgagor's redemption period has elapsed, junior lienors usually have the right to redeem in the order of their priority.

C. Amount Required for Redemption

The amount required for statutory redemption is generally the foreclosure sale price, not the amount of the mortgage debt.

D. Effect of Redemption

1. By the Mortgagor or His Successor

Statutory redemption by the mortgagor or his successor annuls the sale and restores title to the redeemer. Authorities differ, however, as to whether unsatisfied pre-existing liens are revived.

2. By a Junior Lienor

When a junior lienor redeems, he generally receives the rights of the purchaser at the foreclosure sale. Other junior interest holders usually may redeem from the original redemptioner.

E. Waiver

Individual mortgagors may not waive statutory redemption except in two or three jurisdictions. In several states, however, corporate mortgagors may waive their rights because statutory redemption would delay or otherwise impede corporate reorganization or dissolution.

F. Compared to Equity of Redemption

Statutory redemption is often confused with equity of redemption. Although both methods of redemption are designed to protect the mortgagor, they differ significantly. First, equity of redemption developed as a part of our common law and is available in all states. Statutory redemption is a legislative creation that exists in only one-half the states. Second, the mortgagor's equity of redemption is extinguished at foreclosure. His statutory right of redemption arises then. An equity of redemption and a right of statutory redemption, therefore, cannot exist in the same person at the same time. Third, the mortgagor's equity of redemption generally is not extinguished at the end of any specific time. It lasts until terminated by foreclosure. Statutory redemption, however, begins at foreclosure and runs for a specific period set by local law. Fourth, redemption in equity is from the mortgage. Redemption under statutory provision is from the sale. Thus, the amount required for equitable redemption is the amount in default, usually the unpaid balance of the mortgage debt. The amount required for statutory redemption is the foreclosure sale price. Fifth, the right of equity of redemption may not be waived. Statutory redemption, however, may be waived by corporate mortgagors in several states and by individual mortgagors in a few jurisdictions.

G. Criticism of Statutory Redemption

Statutory redemption is often criticized on the ground that it does not really accomplish its intended purpose—to produce realistic bids at the foreclosure sale. *See* United States v. Stadium Apartments, Inc., 425 F.2d 358 (9th Cir.1970) *cert.*

denied 400 U.S. 926, 91 S.Ct. 187 (1970). Many critics go even further and suggest that statutory redemption is counterproductive. The fact that the purchaser must wait for a year or so before receiving the property may dampen bidding by outsiders and thereby depress the sale price. Moreover, this delay and its attendant risks may cause mortgagees to lend less or demand a higher rate of return in states that utilize a statutory redemption period to "protect" mortgagors.

CHAPTER 11

FINANCING COOPERATIVES AND CONDOMINIUMS

I. BACKGROUND

As the population of this country began to crowd our urban centers during the first half of this century it became increasingly difficult for many people to realize the American dream of home ownership. Housing cooperatives and condominiums were developed in large part to meet the public's desire in this area. Both offer the individual the opportunity to acquire a unit in a multi-unit building. (Although most cooperatives and condominiums are residential developments, either form of ownership may be used for a commercial project.)

The cooperative and the condominium pose unique real estate finance problems. These issues are explored in this chapter, but first it is necessary to review the general legal principles underlying each form of development.

II. COOPERATIVES

A. The Cooperative Concept

Cooperative apartments became popular in New York City during the early 1900's and soon spread to other large urban areas. Title to the cooperative apartment building and the land upon which it is located is usually held by a non-profit corporation. Stock in the corporation is allocated among the apartment units based upon their relative size or value. Each cooperative member purchases the number of shares assigned to the apartment he wishes to occupy and then receives a long-term "proprietary" lease to that unit. The rent payable under the lease is his proportionate share of the expenses the corporation incurs in operating the cooperative. Expenses include costs for taxes, insurance, maintenance, management, and debt service.

B. Financing Cooperatives

1. *Construction or Acquisition Financing*

In order to finance the purchase or construction of the cooperative building, the cooperative corporation places a blanket mortgage on the property. This general financing arrangement presents the individual cooperative members with a number of financing problems.

2. *Loans on Individual Units*

Lending institutions generally are reluctant or unable to take an individual member's stock and proprietary lease as security for a long-term loan. Although such loans are more readily available today than they were ten or fifteen years ago, cooperative apartment purchasers still face considerable difficulty in obtaining adequate financing in many areas of the country. As a result, the purchaser of a cooperative apartment often must have enough ready cash to pay for the stock allocated to the unit he wishes to acquire. This generally poses no problem for the first purchaser because the initial price of the stock usually approximates the amount needed for a downpayment on a single family dwelling or a condominium. But, as cooperative members build equity in their stock, subsequent purchasers must either have a large amount of cash on hand or find a seller who is willing to recover his equity in installments over a number of years.

3. *Partial Default on the Blanket Mortgage*

The financial interdependence of the cooperative members is another source of concern. The existence of a single blanket mortgage paid by rent receipts means that if several members fail to pay rent, the cooperative may not have sufficient funds to meet a mortgage loan installment. The entire membership is then faced with foreclosure unless they take action to cure the default. Although reserves and special assessments may be utilized to cover such a contingency, there is always the possibility that available funds will be inadequate and that all cooperative members will be at the mercy of the blanket mortgagee.

III. CONDOMINIUMS

A. The Condominium Concept

Although the cooperative apartment member is more than an ordinary tenant, he does not hold title to his unit. The condominium owner does. This idea of separate ownership of housing units in a multi-unit building is not new. The condominium concept originated in Europe during the Middle Ages, but became popular only recently. Changes in economic, political and social conditions precipitated dramatic condominium growth in this country in the last twenty years. The combination of a land shortage, legislation in each state establishing guidelines for the creation of condominiums, and the willingness of the federal government to insure mortgages on individual condominium units caused condominium developments to spring up in such numbers that they now occupy a significant position in the overall housing picture. As might be expected, the cooperative dwindled in importance as the condominium rose in popularity.

A condominium is created when a developer records a formal declaration that he submits certain property to the local condominium act. The property may consist of a single high rise structure, a number of garden apartment buildings, a series of row houses, or even several single family dwellings. In every case, each condominium unit is identified in the declaration.

The purchaser of a unit receives the fee simple to that unit. He also receives an undivided percentage interest in the common areas of the development as a tenant in common with the other unit owners. The common areas include the land and all the structural parts of the building not included within the description of individual units. An owners association, usually formed as a nonprofit corporation, manages the common areas and facilities.

The concept of separate ownership of part of a building has generated numerous legal problems. Litigation and legislation in the area is ever increasing. In 1977, the National Conference of Commissions on Uniform State Laws approved the Uniform Condominium Act as a means to deal with unsettled condominium issues on a consistent basis throughout the country. Three years later the Commissioners amended and reissued the Act. Whether the 1980 version will find the widespread acceptance that eluded its predecessor is an open question.

B. Financing Condominiums

This book is designed to present the fundamentals of real estate finance, not a detailed analysis of condominium law. Hence, this section treats only the narrow area of condominium financing.

1. Construction Financing

Financing condominium construction is similar to financing subdivision development. In each case the developer obtains a blanket construction mortgage loan to finance the contemplated improvements. When construction is completed and a unit purchaser located, the purchaser obtains a permanent mortgage loan to pay the purchase price of his unit. The developer uses the money he receives from the purchaser to pay a proportionate share of the blanket construction loan. The construction lender in turn executes a partial release of the construction mortgage so that the developer can convey clear title to the unit in question. The end result is that the purchaser holds title to his unit subject only to the lien of the permanent purchase money mortgage. This process is repeated until no units are left in the hands of the developer. Thus, the transition from the construction loan to permanent financing is accomplished in a series of transactions as housing units in the subdivision or condominium are sold.

The condominium construction lender, however, faces a problem the subdivision financer does not. Construction of the condominium building cannot be halted in midstream if the units are not selling well. Further, if the lender executes a partial release as each unit is conveyed, he may end up with a lien on only the least valuable portions of his original security. Many condominium construction lenders, therefore, will not execute any partial releases until the developer has obtained sales contracts for a certain percentage of the units. The lender may also require the developer to have a plan for converting the development into a rental project in the event the units do not sell.

2. Conversion Financing

Owners of rental apartment buildings often use the condominium concept as a means to profitably dispose of their property. (Conversions to cooperatives occur, but are not nearly as common.) The conversion process presents some financing problems. The existing mortgagee may be unwilling to cooperate with the conversion and grant partial releases as the condominium units are sold. In this event, the owner must obtain short term mortgage financing from another source in order to bridge the conversion period. The proceeds of the new mortgage loan are used to pay the original lender. The owner then organizes the condominium and sells the units. The transition from the interim loan to permanent financing is accomplished in the same fashion as described in the preceding subsection on construction financing.

3.   Loans on Individual Units

a.   General

The owner of a condominium unit may obtain financing on his unit in the same manner as the owner of a single family dwelling. *See* Appendix C for a Condominium Rider to a standard mortgage. Thus, there is not the same financial interdependence among condominium owners as exists among cooperative apartment members. If one condominium unit owner defaults in the payment of his mortgage loan, he faces foreclosure alone. The lender does not necessarily have a lien on any other unit. This availability of separate financing of individual units is the most striking advantage of condominium ownership over investment in a cooperative apartment.

b.   Priority vis-a-vis Assessment Liens

Although condominium unit owners are less financially interdependent than are cooperative apartment members, they are far more so than are conventional home owners. This is because they must work together to maintain the condominium common areas. To achieve this objective, the condominium homeowners association makes an assessment against each owner for his share of the expenses of the condominium project. If a unit owner does not pay his assessment, the association receives a statutory lien against his condominium unit. Under many current condominium statutes a lien for unpaid assessments is junior to an existing first mortgage on the unit. The Uniform Condominium Act, however, gives an assessment lien priority over an existing first mortgage for up to six months of unpaid assessments on the ground that such a limited preference is crucial to the financial well-being of the development. U.C.A. § 3–116 (1980 version). Mortgage lenders indirectly benefit from fully-funded maintenance programs because the value of their security is thereby preserved. Moreover, lenders may easily protect themselves against loss of lien priority by requiring the unit owner to escrow funds for assessments just as he must for taxes and insurance.

CHAPTER 12

REFORM

I. THE NEED FOR REFORM

The diverse real estate finance law discussed in the first ten chapters of this book has impeded the free flow of funds for residential and commercial mortgage financing. Because national lenders must vary their procedures to meet a wide variety of state laws, the overall cost of administering mortgage loans is higher than if lenders had but one set of legal principles to follow. In addition, where mortgagees view local law as particularly burdensome, they tend to become more conservative in their lending practices and may even reduce their mortgage investments.

The current judicial foreclosure system is subject to especially heavy criticism. During the lengthy, complex, and expensive court-supervised foreclosure process, mortgage money is tied up and the mortgaged property may deteriorate or be destroyed, vandalized, or milked of its value.

II. REFORM MEASURES

In recent years, proposals to reform the law of real estate finance have been advanced at both the federal and state levels of government.

[207]

A. Federal Action

1. *A Nationwide Foreclosure System*

Federal housing and secondary mortgage market programs are burdened by the absence of uniform state mortgage law. The 93rd Congress, therefore, entertained a bill to establish a standard nationwide procedure for foreclosing mortgages owned, insured, or guaranteed by an instrumentality of the federal government. This proposal, known as the Federal Mortgage Foreclosure Act, provided for nonjudicial foreclosure of all such federally related mortgages by a foreclosure commissioner. H.R. 10688, 93rd Cong., 1st Sess. (1973); S. 2507, 93rd Cong., 1st Sess. (1973). Although the Act was not adopted, it clearly demonstrated Congressional concern about the present fragmented state foreclosure system.

A broad federal foreclosure system still has not been enacted, but Congress recently passed a narrow statute on the subject. The Multifamily Mortgage Foreclosure Act of 1981, 12 U.S.C.A. § 3701 *et seq.*, establishes an out-of-court foreclosure system for certain multifamily mortgages held by HUD. A foreclosure commissioner is designated to conduct the procedure.

2. *Other Federal Statutes*

Certain federal statutes preempting state real estate finance law on nonforeclosure matters are addressed elsewhere in this book. Qualified preemption of state usury law (*see* Ch. 4, p. 79) and of state limitations on the use of alternative mortgage instruments (*see* Ch. 4, p. 72) are two examples.

3. *Preemption of State Mortgage Law in the Courts*

The recent spate of lawsuits brought by federal agencies challenging the applicability of local law to federally owned or insured mortgages is another indication of the federal government's dissatisfaction with current mortgage law. In these cases, the courts have found several state mortgage laws unenforceable against federal agencies on the ground that federal law or policy preempted the field. State statutes establishing a statutory redemption period and limiting deficiency judgments are just two types of local laws that have met this fate.

4. *Standard Mortgage Forms*

Various federal agencies and secondary mortgage market support institutions have brought a measure of uniformity to mortgage law and practice by standardizing mortgage forms. The Federal Housing Administration and the Veterans Administration require that their standard forms be used for mortgage loans they insure or guaranty. In addition, the Federal National Mortgage Association and the Federal Home Loan Mortgage Corporation have developed uniform mortgage instruments with appropriate "riders" to be used for conventional mortgage loans. *See* Appendices A, B, and C.

5. *Further Federal Action*

Piecemeal federal legislation or sporadic litigation of the preemption issue is not an adequate substitute for a uniform mortgage law. Neither is the widespread use of a standard mortgage form. Nonetheless, the Federal Mortgage Foreclosure Act or a similar measure certainly will be reintroduced in Congress. Whether one of these bills is enacted depends in good part on the states. If they can agree on some measure of uniformity in the real estate finance area, the need for further federal action may abate.

B. Uniform Land Transactions Act

1. *General*

The tool to achieve a unified real estate finance structure among the states is available in the form of Article 3 of the Uniform Land Transactions Act ("ULTA"). ULTA is designed to modernize and to make uniform the law of consensual real estate transactions through the adoption of personal property concepts embodied in the Uniform Commercial Code ("U.C.C."). ULTA § 1–102. ULTA is divided into three parts: Article 1 (General Provisions), Article 2 (Contracts and Conveyances), and Article 3 (Secured Transactions). Article 3, which is modeled after Article 9 of the U.C.C., dramatically revises current real estate finance law. Although Article 3 deals in detail with a wide range of land financing problems, the scope of this work permits presentation of only its most significant aspects.

2. *Significant Provisions*

a. Coverage

With a few minor exceptions, Article 3 of ULTA applies to all consensual arrangements designed to create a security interest in realty. ULTA §§ 3–102, 3–104. Thus, installment land contracts are treated the same as mortgages. *See* Ch. 3, pp. 48–52.

b. New Terminology and Concepts

ULTA introduces new U.C.C.-like terminology for traditional real estate financing concepts. Under the Act, mortgages are called "security agreements," mortgagors are termed "debtors," and mortgagees are labelled "secured creditors." ULTA § 3–103.

ULTA also establishes a unique "protected party" status. In the context of Article 3, a protected party is basically an owner who mortgages his residence. ULTA § 1–203. Such individuals receive special treatment in numerous ways. For example, a protected party is given rights at foreclosure not available to mortgagors in general.

c. Rights and Duties Before Foreclosure

ULTA attempts to resolve many of the controversies that may arise between the parties before foreclosure. Article 3 is pro-lender in that it strengthens the mortgagee's security position, but not necessarily to the detriment of mortgagors. Many of the changes in the law incorporated in Article 3 parallel common contractual undertakings and are designed to reduce uncertains that drive up the cost of real estate financing.

The major question in this area concerns the mortgagee's right to take possession and collect rents and profits. You are well aware of the complexity of this issue under existing law. *See* Ch. 8, pp. 142–152. ULTA adopts the intermediate theory thereby permitting the mortgagee to take possession upon the mortgagor's default. The rights and obligations of a mortgage in possession are better defined and less burdensome than under existing law. Moreover, rules are established regarding the mortgagee's right to collect rents, with or without taking possession. The overall effect is two pronged. First, it is easier for the mortgagee to collect rents, take possession, or both. Second, the use of a costly receiver is thereby discouraged. ULTA §§ 3–502 to 3–504.

d. Foreclosure Procedures

The foreclosure provisions of Article 3 contain the reform of greatest interest to the real estate finance community. ULTA §§ 3–505 to 3–513. Although foreclosure by judicial sale is still available in all cases, ULTA establishes power of sale as the preferred method of foreclosure. Notice requirements, however, are more stringent than under existing law. *See* Ch. 10, pp. 188–193.

Two other changes in prior foreclosure law deserve note. First, there is no statutory redemption period under ULTA. Second, the purchaser's title at a power of sale foreclosure conducted pursuant to Article 3 is as marketable as title received at a judicial sale. ULTA §§ 3–511 to 3–513.

3. *Status*

ULTA was originally approved by the National Conference of Commissioners on Uniform State Laws in 1975. Two years later the Commissioners revised several portions of the Act at the behest of the American Bar Association. Although ULTA has generated considerable commentary in the legal literature, at this writing it has not been enacted anywhere. With the passage of time and increased federal involvement in the real estate finance area, the likelihood of widespread adoption of Article 3 is gradually diminishing.

TABLE OF SECONDARY AUTHORITIES

Secondary authorities are listed by chapter, section, and subsection. Four of the sources cited in this table deserve special mention. My general approach to real estate finance has been significantly influenced by two casebooks: Nelson & Whitman, Real Estate Transfer, Finance, and Development Cases and Materials (2d ed. 1981) (hereinafter cited as Nelson & Whitman) and an earlier edition of Penney & Broude, Cases and Materials on Land Financing (2d ed.1977) (hereinafter cited as Penney & Broude). Two other books served as key references in the preparation of this text. The first was G. Osborne, D. Nelson, & D. Whitman, Real Estate Finance Law (1979) (hereinafter cited as Osborne, Nelson, & Whitman) successor to the classic work in the field—Osborne, Handbook on the Law of Mortgages (2d ed.1970) (hereinafter cited as Osborne (2d ed.1970)). The second was a fine practice-oriented book—R. Kratovil & R. Werner, Modern Morgage Law and Practice (2d ed.1981) (hereinafter cited as Kratovil & Werner).

SECONDARY AUTHORITIES

CHAPTER 1. INTRODUCTION

I. A. Osborne, Nelson, & Whitman § 1.1

    B. Kratovil and Werner § 32.01; Osborne, Nelson, & Whitman §§ 5.27, 6.4.

    C. Osborne, §§ 49–63 (2d ed.1970); 5 Tiffany, The Law of Real Property § 1563 (1939).

II. Kane, *The Mortgagee's Option to Purchase Mortgaged Property* in Financing Real Estate During the Inflationary 80s 123 (B. Strum ed.1981) (reference for subsection B. 2. only); Kratovil & Werner §§ 1.2–1.5, 1.7; Osborne §§ 5–10 (2d ed.1970); Osborne, Nelson, & Whitman §§ 1.2–1.4, 1.7, 3.1.

III. Kratovil & Werner §§ 1.6, 1.8; Osborne §§ 13–16 (2d ed.1970); Osborne, Nelson, & Whitman § 1.5.

CHAPTER 2. THE MORTGAGE MARKET

I. A. & B. 1. & 2. Kratovil, Modern Mortgage Law and Practice §§ 207–209 (1972) (hereinafter cited as Kratovil (1972)); Nelson & Whitman 663; Kratovil & Werner §§ 25.05(a)–25.11, 25.35–25.38(a); Osborne, Nelson, & Whitman § 12.1.

        3. a. Hart & Kane, *What Every Lawyer Should Know About Payment and Performance Bonds*, 17 Real Prop.,Prob. & Tr.J. 674 (1982); Kratovil & Werner §§ 25.03–25.03(b)(2), 25.13, 25.17–25.21, 25.27(f)–25.27(f)(5); Livingston, *Current Business Approaches—Commercial Construction Lending*, 13 Real Prob.,Prob. & Tr.J. 791 (1978); Osborne, Nelson, & Whitman § 12.2.

           b. Comment, *Liability of the Institutional Lender for Structural Defects in New Housing*, 35 U.Chi.L.Rev. 739 (1968); Ferguson, *Lender's Liability for Construction Defects*, 11 Real Est. L.J. 310 (1983); Osborne, Nelson, & Whitman § 12.11.

C. & II. Nelson & Whitman 661–663.

III. Axelrod, Berger, & Johnstone, Land Transfer and Finance 83–91 (2d ed.1978); Kratovil & Werner §§ 7.03(d)–7.03(e); Miles, *Housing Finance: Development and Evolution in Mortgage Mar-*

Ch. 2   III.   *kets* in Housing—A Reader 45, 55–65 (Cong. Research Service, Library of Congress, July, 1983) (hereinafter cited as Miles); Osborne, Nelson, & Whitman § 11.1; 4 Rohan, Real Estate Financing §§ 3.01–3.02 (1983) (hereinafter cited as Rohan); U.S. Dept. of Hous. & Urb. Dev. Report, Housing in the Seventies 3–30 to 3–38, 5–3 to 5–11, 5–21 to 5–26 (hereinafter cited as HUD Report).

          IV.   Brannon, *Enforceability of Mortgage Loan Commitments*, 18 Real Prop., Prob. & Tr.J. 724 (1983); Groot, *Specific Performance of Contracts to Provide Permanent Financing*, 60 Cornell L.Rev. 718 (1974); Kratovil & Werner §§ 4.01–4.06; Osborne, Nelson, & Whitman § 12.3; Penney & Broude 938–939 (note 2); 3 Powell on Real Property ¶ 441.1 (1981) (hereinafter cited as Powell).

          V.   Kratovil & Werner §§ 29.04–29.04(c), 33.01–33.10(c); Lance, *Balancing Private and Public Initiatives in the Mortgage-Backed Security Market*, 18 Real Prop., Prob. & Tr.J. 426 (1983); Strine, *New Commercial Devices—Mortgage-Backed Securities*, 13 Real Prop., Prob. & Tr.J. 1011 (1978).

          VI.   A.   4C Rohan §§ 9.01–9.03.

                 B.   Gunning, *The Wrap-Around Mortgage . . . Friend or U.F.O.?* 2 Real Est. Rev. 35 (Summer 1972); Kratovil & Werner §§ 24.11–24.11(f); Note, *Wrap-Around Financing: A Technique for Skirting the Usury Laws?*, 1972 Duke L.J. 785; 4C Rohan §§ 10.01–10.08.

         VII.   A.   HUD Report 1–14 to 1–24, 4–1 to 4–109; Milgram, *Housing the Urban Poor: Urban Housing Assistance Programs* in Housing—A Reader 114 (Cong. Research Service, Library of Congress, July, 1983).

                 B.   HUD Report 3–48 to 3–53; Miles at 61; Nelson & Whitman 714–723 (notes 1–7); Osborne, Nelson, & Whitman § 11.2; 4 Rohan § 3.03; Rothman, *Mortgages Insured by FHA Will Fluctuate With Market*, 42 Cong.Q.Weekly Report 20 (Jan. 7, 1984).

Ch. 2   VII.   C.   HUD Report 3–39 to 3–48; Miles 59–61; Osborne, Nelson, & Whitman § 11.3.

D.   1.   P. Barron, Federal Regulation of Real Estate 10–1 to 10–61 (Rev.ed.1983 & Supp.1983) (hereinafter cited as Barron); D. Epstein & S. Nickles, Consumer Law in a Nutshell 82–85, 138–146, 198–201 (2d ed. 1981) (hereinafter cited as Epstein & Nickles).

2.   Barron 3–1 to 3–46; Catalina, *Interstate Land Sales—Tightening Consumer Protection*, 10 Real Est.L.J. 72 (1981); Comment, *The Interstate Land Sales Full Disclosure Act: An Analysis of Administrative Policies Implemented in the Years 1968–1975*, 26 Cath.U.L.Rev. 348 (1977); Epstein & Nickles 146–149; Malloy, *The Interstate Land Sales Full Disclosure Act: Its Requirements, Consequences, and Implications for Persons Participating in Real Estate Development*, 24 B.C.L. Rev. 118 (1983); Report, *Exemptions from the Registration Requirements of the Interstate Land Sales Full Disclosure Act*, 15 Real Prop., Prob. & Tr.J. 334 (1980).

3.   Baram & Miyares, *Managing Flood Risk: Technical Uncertainty in the National Flood Insurance Program*, 7 Colum.J.Envtl.L. 129 (1982); Tierney, *National Flood Insurance Program: Exploration and Legal Implications*, 8 Urb.Law. 279 (1976).

4.   Barron 2–1 to 2–54; Epstein & Nickles 149–151; Field, *RESPA in a Nutshell*, 11 Real Prop., Prob. & Tr.J. 447 (1976); 3 Powell ¶ 475.6A.

5.   Barron 11–1 to 11–7; Lechner, *National Banks and State Anti-Redlining Laws: Has Congress Preempted the Field?* 99 Banking L.J. 388 (1982); Note, *The Home Mortgage Disclosure Act of 1975: Will it Protect Urban Consumers from Redlining*, 12 N.Eng.L.Rev. 957 (1977).

CHAPTER 3. REAL ESTATE FINANCING DEVICES

I.   A.   Kratovil & Werner §§ 19.01–19.09; Osborne, Nelson, & Whitman §§ 1.1, 9.1.

SECONDARY AUTHORITIES

SECONDARY AUTHORITIES

SECONDARY AUTHORITIES

SECONDARY AUTHORITIES

CHAPTER 5. THE MORTGAGED PROPERTY

CHAPTER 6. TRANSFER OF THE MORTGAGOR'S INTEREST

Ch. 6   II.   A. & B.   Dunn & Nowinski, *Enforcement of Due-on-Transfer Clauses: An Update*, 16 Real Prop., Prob. & Tr. J. 291 (1981); Osborne, Nelson, & Whitman §§ 5.21–5.26; Note, *Due-on-Sale Clauses: Separating Social Interests from Individual Interests*, 35 Vand.L.Rev. 357 (1982); Report, *Enforcement of Due-on-Transfer Clauses*, 13 Real Prop., Prob. & Tr.J. 891 (1978); Volkmer, *The Application of the Restraints on Alienation Doctrine to Real Property Security Interests*, 58 Iowa L.Rev. 747 (1973).

           C., D., & E.   Barad & Layden, *Due-on-Sale Law as Preempted by the Garn-St. Germain Act*, 12 Real Est.L.J. 138 (1983); Coleman, *Federal Preemption of State Law Prohibitions on the Exercise of Due-on-Sale Clauses*, 100 Banking L.J. 772 (1983); Geier, *Due-on-Sale Clauses under the Garn-St. Germain Depository Institutions Act of 1982*, 17 U.S.F.L.Rev. 355 (1983); Nelson & Whitman, *Congressional Preemption of Mortgage Due-on-Sale Law: An Analysis of the Garn-St. Germain Act*, 35 Hastings L.J. 241 (1983); FHLBB Regulations, *Preemption of State Due-on-sale Laws*, 48 Fed.Regis. 21554–21563 (1983).

III.   See sources cited in section II above.

IV.   Osborne § 251 (2d ed.1970).

CHAPTER 7. TRANSFER OF THE MORTGAGEE'S INTEREST

I. & II. A. & B. Osborne, Nelson, & Whitman § 5.27–5.28; 3 Powell ¶ 455.

        C.   Kratovil & Werner § 32.02; Osborne, Nelson, & Whitman § 5.34.

        D.   Osborne, Nelson, & Whitman §§ 5.27, 11.3.

III.   Kratovil & Werner §§ 32.05–32.06; Osborne §§ 227–228, 231 (2d ed.1970); Osborne, Nelson, & Whitman §§ 5.27–5.33.

IV.   Annot., 89 A.L.R. 171 (1934); Kratovil & Werner §§ 34.01–34.01(d); Osborne §§ 234–237 (2d ed.1970); Osborne, Nelson, & Whitman § 5.33–5.34.

SECONDARY AUTHORITIES

CHAPTER 8. RIGHTS AND DUTIES AFTER DEFAULT AND BEFORE FORECLOSURE

Ch. 9 III. D.   3.   *teenth Amendment Guarantees,* 26 Cath.U.L.Rev. 129 (1976); Osborne, Nelson, & Whitman § 12.5.

          4.   Comment, *Mechanics Liens: The "Stop Notice" Comes to Washington,* 49 Wash.L.Rev. 685 (1974); Note, *Lien Rights and Construction Lending: Responsibilities and Liabilities in Florida,* 29 Fla.L.Rev. 411 (1977); Osborne, Nelson, & Whitman § 12.6.

      E.   1.   Glenn §§ 434–435.

          2.   Kratovil §§ 422–429 (1972); 3 Powell ¶¶ 495–496.

      F.   Osborne, Nelson, & Whitman § 7.13.

      G.   1.   Kratovil & Werner §§ 16.04, 34.05(h); Osborne, Nelson, & Whitman §§ 10.10, 10.15; Walsh § 55.

          2.   Glenn §§ 289–292.2, 294.1–295; Osborne, Nelson, & Whitman §§ 10.09–10.11; Walsh § 56.

          3.   Glenn §§ 294, 296; Kratovil & Werner § 16.04.

CHAPTER 10. FORECLOSURE

I.   Kratovil & Werner § 41.09(c); 3 Powell ¶ 462.

II.   Osborne, Nelson, & Whitman §§ 6.9, 6.12.

III.   Osborne, Nelson, & Whitman § 7.11.

      A.   1.   Kratovil & Werner § 41.09(c); Osborne, Nelson, & Whitman §§ 7.12, 7.14.

          2.   Nelson & Whitman 614–616 (notes 1–3); Osborne, Nelson, & Whitman § 8.14.

          3.   Annot., 40 A.L.R.2d 1262 (1955); Bagley, *The Soldiers' and Sailors' Civil Relief Act—A Survey,* 45 Mil.L. Rev. 1 (1969); Kratovil & Werner §§ 41.05–41.05(c); *Military and Civil Defense,* 54 Am.Jur.2d §§ 326–331 (1971); Osborne, Nelson, & Whitman §§ 8.8–8.10.

          4.   Kratovil & Werner § 20.05; Osborne, Nelson, & Whitman § 7.12.

          5.   Osborne, Nelson, & Whitman § 7.13.

   B. & C.   Kratovil & Werner §§ 41.09(h)–41.09(*o*); Osborne, Nelson, & Whitman § 7.16; 3 Powell ¶ 466; Washburn, *The Judicial and Legislative Response to Price Inadequacy in Mortgage Foreclosure Sales,* 53 S.Cal.L.Rev. 843 (1980).

      D.   1.   Glenn § 94; Osborne, Nelson, & Whitman § 7.17.

          2.   Osborne, Nelson, & Whitman § 7.15.

          3.   Glenn § 94.1; Kratovil & Werner § 41.09(m).

SECONDARY AUTHORITIES

Ch. 10 III. D.   4.   Kratovil & Werner § 41.16.

       E.   3 Powell ¶ 467; Osborne, Nelson, & Whitman §§ 7.31–7.32; Walsh § 79.

       F.   Osborne, Nelson, & Whitman §§ 8.1, 8.3; Walsh § 77.

    IV.   Kratovil & Werner §§ 41.08–41.08(a); Osborne, Nelson, & Whitman § 7.19; 3 Powell ¶ 468.

       A.   Kratovil & Werner §§ 41.08–41.08(c), 41.08(e)–41.08(p); Osborne §§ 343–344; Osborne, Nelson, & Whitman §§ 7.19–7.22; 3 Powell ¶ 468.

       B.   Comment, *Power of Sale Foreclosure After Fuentes*, 40 U.Chi.L.Rev. 206 (1972); Osborne, Nelson, & Whitman §§ 7.23–7.30; Pedowitz, *Current Developments in Summary Foreclosure*, 9 Real Prop., Prob. & Tr.J. 421, 425–431 (1974).

    V.   Osborne, Nelson, & Whitman §§ 7.9–7.10; Osborne §§ 314–315 (2d ed.1970); 3 Powell § 469.

    VI.   Kratovil & Werner §§ 42.06–42.17; Osborne § 8 (2d ed. 1970); Osborne, Nelson, & Whitman §§ 8.4–8.7.

CHAPTER 11. FINANCING COOPERATIVES AND CONDOMINIUMS

I.–III.   Garfinkel, *The Uniform Condominium Act*, 28 Prac.Law. 43 (Dec. 1, 1982); King, *Problems of Financing Condominiums*, 24 Bus.Law. 445 (1969); Kratovil & Werner §§ 26.01–26.14; Pfeiler, *Condominium Financing: Some Legal Basics*, 38 U.S. League of Sav. Ass'n Legal Bull. 249 (1972); Osborne, Nelson, & Whitman §§ 13.1–13.6; 4B Powell ¶¶ 631–633.36[7], 633.44A–633.52; 633.54–633.59; P. Rohan & M. Reskin, Condominium Law and Practice (1983); P. Rohan & M. Reskin, Cooperative Housing Law and Practice (1983); Thomas, *The New Uniform Condominium Act*, 64 A.B.A.J. 1370 (1978); Uniform Condominium Act prefatory note and § 3–116 comment 2 (1980 version).

CHAPTER 12. REFORM

I. & II.   A.   1.–3.   Madway & Pearlman, *Mortgage Forms and Foreclosure Practices: Time for Reform*, 9 Real Prop., Prob. & Tr.J. 560 (1974); Osborne, Nelson, & Whitman § 11.6; Pedowitz, *Current Developments in Summary Foreclosure*, 9 Real Prop., Prob. & Tr.J. 421 (1974); Report, *Cost and Time Factors in Fore-*

Ch. 12   I. & II.   A.   1.–3.   *closure of Mortgages*, 3 Real Prop., Prob. & Tr.J. 413
(1968).

4.   Kratovil & Werner §§ 6.02, 6.22(b)–6.24(a).

B.   Bruce, *Mortgage Law Reform Under the Uniform
Land Transactions Act*, 64 Geo.L.J. 1245 (1976);
Comment, *ULTA and Non-Judicial Mortgage Fore-
closure in Texas*, 12 St. Mary's L.J. 1104 (1981);
Pedowitz, *Mortgage Foreclosure Under the Uniform
Land Transactions Act (As Amended)*, 6 Real Est.
L.J. 179 (1978);   Uniform Land Transactions Act pref-
atory note, introductory note to Article 3, & com-
ments to §§ 3–101 to 3–513.

*

APPENDIX A

STANDARD NOTE AND MORTGAGE FORMS

The Federal National Mortgage Association (FNMA) and the Federal Home Loan Mortgage Corporation (FHLMC) have developed uniform note and mortgage instruments for use throughout the country. *See* Ch. 12, pp. 209–210. The FNMA/FHLMC mortgage form contains a "uniform covenants" section which is the same in all states and a "nonuniform covenants" section which varies somewhat from jurisdiction to jurisdiction in order to accommodate minor differences in local law. Following are the FNMA/FHLMC uniform note and mortgage instruments used in Indiana.

APPENDIX A

NOTE

...., 19.........   ...., ...
                                                                                          [City]   [State]

....
[Property Address]

1. BORROWER'S PROMISE TO PAY

In return for a loan that I have received, I promise to pay U.S. $.. (this amount is called "principal"), plus interest, to the order of the Lender. The Lender is ....
.... I understand that the Lender may transfer this Note. The Lender or anyone who takes this Note by transfer and who is entitled to receive payments under this Note is called the "Note Holder."

2. INTEREST

Interest will be charged on unpaid principal until the full amount of principal has been paid. I will pay interest at a yearly rate of ....%.

The interest rate required by this Section 2 is the rate I will pay both before and after any default described in Section 6(B) of this Note.

3. PAYMENTS

(A) Time and Place of Payments

I will pay principal and interest by making payments every month.

I will make my monthly payments on the .... day of each month beginning on ...., 19......... I will make these payments every month until I have paid all of the principal and interest and any other charges described below that I may owe under this Note. My monthly payments will be applied to interest before principal. If, on ...., ..., I still owe amounts under this Note, I will pay those amounts in full on that date, which is called the "maturity date."

I will make my monthly payments at ....
.... or at a different place if required by the Note Holder.

(B) Amount of Monthly Payments

My monthly payment will be in the amount of U.S. $..

4. BORROWER'S RIGHT TO PREPAY

I have the right to make payments of principal at any time before they are due. A payment of principal only is known as a "prepayment." When I make a prepayment, I will tell the Note Holder in writing that I am doing so.

I may make a full prepayment or partial prepayments without paying any prepayment charge. The Note Holder will use all of my prepayments to reduce the amount of principal that I owe under this Note. If I make a partial prepayment, there will be no changes in the due date or in the amount of my monthly payment unless the Note Holder agrees in writing to those changes.

5. LOAN CHARGES

If a law, which applies to this loan and which sets maximum loan charges, is finally interpreted so that the interest or other loan charges collected or to be collected in connection with this loan exceed the permitted limits, then: (i) any such loan charge shall be reduced by the amount necessary to reduce the charge to the permitted limit; and (ii) any sums already collected from me which exceeded permitted limits will be refunded to me. The Note Holder may choose to make this refund by reducing the principal I owe under this Note or by making a direct payment to me. If a refund reduces principal, the reduction will be treated as a partial prepayment.

6. BORROWER'S FAILURE TO PAY AS REQUIRED

(A) Late Charge for Overdue Payments

If the Note Holder has not received the full amount of any monthly payment by the end of .... calendar days after the date it is due, I will pay a late charge to the Note Holder. The amount of the charge will be ....% of my overdue payment of principal and interest. I will pay this late charge promptly but only once on each late payment.

(B) Default

If I do not pay the full amount of each monthly payment on the date it is due, I will be in default.

(C) Notice of Default

If I am in default, the Note Holder may send me a written notice telling me that if I do not pay the overdue amount by a certain date, the Note Holder may require me to pay immediately the full amount of principal which has not been paid and all the interest that I owe on that amount. That date must be at least 30 days after the date on which the notice is delivered or mailed to me.

(D) No Waiver By Note Holder

Even if, at a time when I am in default, the Note Holder does not require me to pay immediately in full as described above, the Note Holder will still have the right to do so if I am in default at a later time.

(E) Payment of Note Holder's Costs and Expenses

If the Note Holder has required me to pay immediately in full as described above, the Note Holder will have the right to be paid back by me for all of its costs and expenses in enforcing this Note to the extent not prohibited by applicable law. Those expenses include, for example, reasonable attorneys' fees.

MULTISTATE FIXED RATE NOTE—Single Family—**FNMA/FHLMC UNIFORM INSTRUMENT**   Form 3200 12/83

STANDARD FORMS

7. GIVING OF NOTICES

Unless applicable law requires a different method, any notice that must be given to me under this Note will be given by delivering it or by mailing it by first class mail to me at the Property Address above or at a different address if I give the Note Holder a notice of my different address.

Any notice that must be given to the Note Holder under this Note will be given by mailing it by first class mail to the Note Holder at the address stated in Section 3(A) above or at a different address if I am given a notice of that different address.

8. OBLIGATIONS OF PERSONS UNDER THIS NOTE

If more than one person signs this Note, each person is fully and personally obligated to keep all of the promises made in this Note, including the promise to pay the full amount owed. Any person who is a guarantor, surety or endorser of this Note is also obligated to do these things. Any person who takes over these obligations, including the obligations of a guarantor, surety or endorser of this Note, is also obligated to keep all of the promises made in this Note. The Note Holder may enforce its rights under this Note against each person individually or against all of us together. This means that any one of us may be required to pay all of the amounts owed under this Note.

9. WAIVERS

I and any other person who has obligations under this Note waive the rights of presentment and notice of dishonor. "Presentment" means the right to require the Note Holder to demand payment of amounts due. "Notice of dishonor" means the right to require the Note Holder to give notice to other persons that amounts due have not been paid.

10. UNIFORM SECURED NOTE

This Note is a uniform instrument with limited variations in some jurisdictions. In addition to the protections given to the Note Holder under this Note, a Mortgage, Deed of Trust or Security Deed (the "Security Instrument"), dated the same date as this Note, protects the Note Holder from possible losses which might result if I do not keep the promises which I make in this Note. That Security Instrument describes how and under what conditions I may be required to make immediate payment in full of all amounts I owe under this Note. Some of those conditions are described as follows:

Transfer of the Property or a Beneficial Interest in Borrower. If all or any part of the Property or any interest in it is sold or transferred (or if a beneficial interest in Borrower is sold or transferred and Borrower is not a natural person) without Lender's prior written consent, Lender may, at its option, require immediate payment in full of all sums secured by this Security Instrument. However, this option shall not be exercised by Lender if exercise is prohibited by federal law as of the date of this Security Instrument.

If Lender exercises this option, Lender shall give Borrower notice of acceleration. The notice shall provide a period of not less than 30 days from the date the notice is delivered or mailed within which Borrower must pay all sums secured by this Security Instrument. If Borrower fails to pay these sums prior to the expiration of this period, Lender may invoke any remedies permitted by this Security Instrument without further notice or demand on Borrower.

WITNESS THE HAND(S) AND SEAL(S) OF THE UNDERSIGNED.

....(Seal)
-Borrower

....(Seal)
-Borrower

..../......................(Seal)
-Borrower

[Sign Original Only]
(D 1258)

APPENDIX A

MORTGAGE

THIS MORTGAGE ("Security Instrument") is given on ....,
19......... The mortgagor is ....
.... ("Borrower"). This Security Instrument is given to ....
...., which is organized and existing
under the laws of ...., and whose address is ....
.... ("Lender").
Borrower owes Lender the principal sum of ....
.... Dollars (U.S. $.................................). This debt is evidenced by Borrower's note
dated the same date as this Security Instrument ("Note"), which provides for monthly payments, with the full debt, if not
paid earlier, due and payable on .... This Security Instrument
secures to Lender: (a) the repayment of the debt evidenced by the Note, with interest, and all renewals, extensions and
modifications; (b) the payment of all other sums, with interest, advanced under paragraph 7 to protect the security of this
Security Instrument; and (c) the performance of Borrower's covenants and agreements under this Security Instrument and
the Note. For this purpose, Borrower does hereby mortgage, grant and convey to Lender the following described property
located in .... County, Indiana:

which has the address of ...., ...,
                                                     [Street]   [City]
Indiana .... ("Property Address");
            [Zip Code]

TOGETHER WITH all the improvements now or hereafter erected on the property, and all easements, rights,
appurtenances, rents, royalties, mineral, oil and gas rights and profits, water rights and stock and all fixtures now or
hereafter a part of the property. All replacements and additions shall also be covered by this Security Instrument. All of the
foregoing is referred to in this Security Instrument as the "Property."

BORROWER COVENANTS that Borrower is lawfully seised of the estate hereby conveyed and has the right to
mortgage, grant and convey the Property and that the Property is unencumbered, except for encumbrances of record.
Borrower warrants and will defend generally the title to the Property against all claims and demands, subject to any
encumbrances of record.

THIS SECURITY INSTRUMENT combines uniform covenants for national use and non-uniform covenants with
limited variations by jurisdiction to constitute a uniform security instrument covering real property.

INDIANA—Single Family—FNMA/FHLMC UNIFORM INSTRUMENT   Form 3015 12/83

STANDARD FORMS

UNIFORM COVENANTS. Borrower and Lender covenant and agree as follows:

1. Payment of Principal and Interest; Prepayment and Late Charges. Borrower shall promptly pay when due the principal of and interest on the debt evidenced by the Note and any prepayment and late charges due under the Note.

2. Funds for Taxes and Insurance. Subject to applicable law or to a written waiver by Lender, Borrower shall pay to Lender on the day monthly payments are due under the Note, until the Note is paid in full, a sum ("Funds") equal to one-twelfth of: (a) yearly taxes and assessments which may attain priority over this Security Instrument; (b) yearly leasehold payments or ground rents on the Property, if any; (c) yearly hazard insurance premiums; and (d) yearly mortgage insurance premiums, if any. These items are called "escrow items." Lender may estimate the Funds due on the basis of current data and reasonable estimates of future escrow items.

The Funds shall be held in an institution the deposits or accounts of which are insured or guaranteed by a federal or state agency (including Lender if Lender is such an institution). Lender shall apply the Funds to pay the escrow items. Lender may not charge for holding and applying the Funds, analyzing the account or verifying the escrow items, unless Lender pays Borrower interest on the Funds and applicable law permits Lender to make such a charge. Borrower and Lender may agree in writing that interest shall be paid on the Funds. Unless an agreement is made or applicable law requires interest to be paid, Lender shall not be required to pay Borrower any interest or earnings on the Funds. Lender shall give to Borrower, without charge, an annual accounting of the Funds showing credits and debits to the Funds and the purpose for which each debit to the Funds was made. The Funds are pledged as additional security for the sums secured by this Security Instrument.

If the amount of the Funds held by Lender, together with the future monthly payments of Funds payable prior to the due dates of the escrow items, shall exceed the amount required to pay the escrow items when due, the excess shall be, at Borrower's option, either promptly repaid to Borrower or credited to Borrower on monthly payments of Funds. If the amount of the Funds held by Lender is not sufficient to pay the escrow items when due, Borrower shall pay to Lender any amount necessary to make up the deficiency in one or more payments as required by Lender.

Upon payment in full of all sums secured by this Security Instrument, Lender shall promptly refund to Borrower any Funds held by Lender. If under paragraph 19 the Property is sold or acquired by Lender, Lender shall apply, no later than immediately prior to the sale of the Property or its acquisition by Lender, any Funds held by Lender at the time of application as a credit against the sums secured by this Security Instrument.

3. Application of Payments. Unless applicable law provides otherwise, all payments received by Lender under paragraphs 1 and 2 shall be applied: first, to late charges due under the Note; second, to prepayment charges due under the Note; third, to amounts payable under paragraph 2; fourth, to interest due; and last, to principal due.

4. Charges; Liens. Borrower shall pay all taxes, assessments, charges, fines and impositions attributable to the Property which may attain priority over this Security Instrument, and leasehold payments or ground rents, if any. Borrower shall pay these obligations in the manner provided in paragraph 2, or if not paid in that manner, Borrower shall pay them on time directly to the person owed payment. Borrower shall promptly furnish to Lender all notices of amounts to be paid under this paragraph. If Borrower makes these payments directly, Borrower shall promptly furnish to Lender receipts evidencing the payments.

Borrower shall promptly discharge any lien which has priority over this Security Instrument unless Borrower: (a) agrees in writing to the payment of the obligation secured by the lien in a manner acceptable to Lender; (b) contests in good faith the lien by, or defends against enforcement of the lien in, legal proceedings which in the Lender's opinion operate to prevent the enforcement of the lien or forfeiture of any part of the Property; or (c) secures from the holder of the lien an agreement satisfactory to Lender subordinating the lien to this Security Instrument. If Lender determines that any part of the Property is subject to a lien which may attain priority over this Security Instrument, Lender may give Borrower a notice identifying the lien. Borrower shall satisfy the lien or take one or more of the actions set forth above within 10 days of the giving of notice.

5. Hazard Insurance. Borrower shall keep the improvements now existing or hereafter erected on the Property insured against loss by fire, hazards included within the term "extended coverage" and any other hazards for which Lender requires insurance. This insurance shall be maintained in the amounts and for the periods that Lender requires. The insurance carrier providing the insurance shall be chosen by Borrower subject to Lender's approval which shall not be unreasonably withheld.

All insurance policies and renewals shall be acceptable to Lender and shall include a standard mortgage clause. Lender shall have the right to hold the policies and renewals. If Lender requires, Borrower shall promptly give to Lender all receipts of paid premiums and renewal notices. In the event of loss, Borrower shall give prompt notice to the insurance carrier and Lender. Lender may make proof of loss if not made promptly by Borrower.

Unless Lender and Borrower otherwise agree in writing, insurance proceeds shall be applied to restoration or repair of the Property damaged, if the restoration or repair is economically feasible and Lender's security is not lessened. If the restoration or repair is not economically feasible or Lender's security would be lessened, the insurance proceeds shall be applied to the sums secured by this Security Instrument, whether or not then due, with any excess paid to Borrower. If Borrower abandons the Property, or does not answer within 30 days a notice from Lender that the insurance carrier has offered to settle a claim, then Lender may collect the insurance proceeds. Lender may use the proceeds to repair or restore the Property or to pay sums secured by this Security Instrument, whether or not then due. The 30-day period will begin when the notice is given.

Unless Lender and Borrower otherwise agree in writing, any application of proceeds to principal shall not extend or postpone the due date of the monthly payments referred to in paragraphs 1 and 2 or change the amount of the payments. If under paragraph 19 the Property is acquired by Lender, Borrower's right to any insurance policies and proceeds resulting from damage to the Property prior to the acquisition shall pass to Lender to the extent of the sums secured by this Security Instrument immediately prior to the acquisition.

6. Preservation and Maintenance of Property; Leaseholds. Borrower shall not destroy, damage or substantially change the Property, allow the Property to deteriorate or commit waste. If this Security Instrument is on a leasehold, Borrower shall comply with the provisions of the lease, and if Borrower acquires fee title to the Property, the leasehold and fee title shall not merge unless Lender agrees to the merger in writing.

7. Protection of Lender's Rights in the Property; Mortgage Insurance. If Borrower fails to perform the covenants and agreements contained in this Security Instrument, or there is a legal proceeding that may significantly affect Lender's rights in the Property (such as a proceeding in bankruptcy, probate, for condemnation or to enforce laws or regulations), then Lender may do and pay for whatever is necessary to protect the value of the Property and Lender's rights in the Property. Lender's actions may include paying any sums secured by a lien which has priority over this Security

APPENDIX A

Instrument, appearing in court, paying reasonable attorneys' fees and entering on the Property to make repairs. Although Lender may take action under this paragraph 7, Lender does not have to do so.

Any amounts disbursed by Lender under this paragraph 7 shall become additional debt of Borrower secured by this Security Instrument. Unless Borrower and Lender agree to other terms of payment, these amounts shall bear interest from the date of disbursement at the Note rate and shall be payable, with interest, upon notice from Lender to Borrower requesting payment.

If Lender required mortgage insurance as a condition of making the loan secured by this Security Instrument, Borrower shall pay the premiums required to maintain the insurance in effect until such time as the requirement for the insurance terminates in accordance with Borrower's and Lender's written agreement or applicable law.

8. Inspection. Lender or its agent may make reasonable entries upon and inspections of the Property. Lender shall give Borrower notice at the time of or prior to an inspection specifying reasonable cause for the inspection.

9. Condemnation. The proceeds of any award or claim for damages, direct or consequential, in connection with any condemnation or other taking of any part of the Property, or for conveyance in lieu of condemnation, are hereby assigned and shall be paid to Lender.

In the event of a total taking of the Property, the proceeds shall be applied to the sums secured by this Security Instrument, whether or not then due, with any excess paid to Borrower. In the event of a partial taking of the Property, unless Borrower and Lender otherwise agree in writing, the sums secured by this Security Instrument shall be reduced by the amount of the proceeds multiplied by the following fraction: (a) the total amount of the sums secured immediately before the taking, divided by (b) the fair market value of the Property immediately before the taking. Any balance shall be paid to Borrower.

If the Property is abandoned by Borrower, or if, after notice by Lender to Borrower that the condemnor offers to make an award or settle a claim for damages, Borrower fails to respond to Lender within 30 days after the date the notice is given, Lender is authorized to collect and apply the proceeds, at its option, either to restoration or repair of the Property or to the sums secured by this Security Instrument, whether or not then due.

Unless Lender and Borrower otherwise agree in writing, any application of proceeds to principal shall not extend or postpone the due date of the monthly payments referred to in paragraphs 1 and 2 or change the amount of such payments.

10. Borrower Not Released; Forbearance By Lender Not a Waiver. Extension of the time for payment or modification of amortization of the sums secured by this Security Instrument granted by Lender to any successor in interest of Borrower shall not operate to release the liability of the original Borrower or Borrower's successors in interest. Lender shall not be required to commence proceedings against any successor in interest or refuse to extend time for payment or otherwise modify amortization of the sums secured by this Security Instrument by reason of any demand made by the original Borrower or Borrower's successors in interest. Any forbearance by Lender in exercising any right or remedy shall not be a waiver of or preclude the exercise of any right or remedy.

11. Successors and Assigns Bound; Joint and Several Liability; Co-signers. The covenants and agreements of this Security Instrument shall bind and benefit the successors and assigns of Lender and Borrower, subject to the provisions of paragraph 17. Borrower's covenants and agreements shall be joint and several. Any Borrower who co-signs this Security Instrument but does not execute the Note: (a) is co-signing this Security Instrument only to mortgage, grant and convey that Borrower's interest in the Property under the terms of this Security Instrument; (b) is not personally obligated to pay the sums secured by this Security Instrument; and (c) agrees that Lender and any other Borrower may agree to extend, modify, forbear or make any accommodations with regard to the terms of this Security Instrument or the Note without that Borrower's consent.

12. Loan Charges. If the loan secured by this Security Instrument is subject to a law which sets maximum loan charges, and that law is finally interpreted so that the interest or other loan charges collected or to be collected in connection with the loan exceed the permitted limits, then: (a) any such loan charge shall be reduced by the amount necessary to reduce the charge to the permitted limit; and (b) any sums already collected from Borrower which exceeded permitted limits will be refunded to Borrower. Lender may choose to make this refund by reducing the principal owed under the Note or by making a direct payment to Borrower. If a refund reduces principal, the reduction will be treated as a partial prepayment without any prepayment charge under the Note.

13. Legislation Affecting Lender's Rights. If enactment or expiration of applicable laws has the effect of rendering any provision of the Note or this Security Instrument unenforceable according to its terms, Lender, at its option, may require immediate payment in full of all sums secured by this Security Instrument and may invoke any remedies permitted by paragraph 19. If Lender exercises this option, Lender shall take the steps specified in the second paragraph of paragraph 17.

14. Notices. Any notice to Borrower provided for in this Security Instrument shall be given by delivering it or by mailing it by first class mail unless applicable law requires use of another method. The notice shall be directed to the Property Address or any other address Borrower designates by notice to Lender. Any notice to Lender shall be given by first class mail to Lender's address stated herein or any other address Lender designates by notice to Borrower. Any notice provided for in this Security Instrument shall be deemed to have been given to Borrower or Lender when given as provided in this paragraph.

15. Governing Law; Severability. This Security Instrument shall be governed by federal law and the law of the jurisdiction in which the Property is located. In the event that any provision or clause of this Security Instrument or the Note conflicts with applicable law, such conflict shall not affect other provisions of this Security Instrument or the Note which can be given effect without the conflicting provision. To this end the provisions of this Security Instrument and the Note are declared to be severable.

16. Borrower's Copy. Borrower shall be given one conformed copy of the Note and of this Security Instrument.

17. Transfer of the Property or a Beneficial Interest in Borrower. If all or any part of the Property or any interest in it is sold or transferred (or if a beneficial interest in Borrower is sold or transferred and Borrower is not a natural person) without Lender's prior written consent, Lender may, at its option, require immediate payment in full of all sums secured by this Security Instrument. However, this option shall not be exercised by Lender if exercise is prohibited by federal law as of the date of this Security Instrument.

If Lender exercises this option, Lender shall give Borrower notice of acceleration. The notice shall provide a period of not less than 30 days from the date the notice is delivered or mailed within which Borrower must pay all sums secured by this Security Instrument. If Borrower fails to pay these sums prior to the expiration of this period, Lender may invoke any remedies permitted by this Security Instrument without further notice or demand on Borrower.

18. Borrower's Right to Reinstate. If Borrower meets certain conditions, Borrower shall have the right to have enforcement of this Security Instrument discontinued at any time prior to the earlier of: (a) 5 days (or such other period as

STANDARD FORMS

applicable law may specify for reinstatement) before sale of the Property pursuant to any power of sale contained in this Security Instrument; or (b) entry of a judgment enforcing this Security Instrument. Those conditions are that Borrower: (a) pays Lender all sums which then would be due under this Security Instrument and the Note had no acceleration occurred; (b) cures any default of any other covenants or agreements; (c) pays all expenses incurred in enforcing this Security Instrument, including, but not limited to, reasonable attorneys' fees; and (d) takes such action as Lender may reasonably require to assure that the lien of this Security Instrument, Lender's rights in the Property and Borrower's · obligation to pay the sums secured by this Security Instrument shall continue unchanged. Upon reinstatement by Borrower, this Security Instrument and the obligations secured hereby shall remain fully effective as if no acceleration had occurred. However, this right to reinstate shall not apply in the case of acceleration under paragraphs 13 or 17.

NON-UNIFORM COVENANTS. Borrower and Lender further covenant and agree as follows:

19. Acceleration; Remedies. Lender shall give notice to Borrower prior to acceleration following Borrower's breach of any covenant or agreement in this Security Instrument (but not prior to acceleration under paragraphs 13 and 17 unless applicable law provides otherwise). The notice shall specify: (a) the default; (b) the action required to cure the default; (c) a date, not less than 30 days from the date the notice is given to Borrower, by which the default must be cured; and (d) that failure to cure the default on or before the date specified in the notice may result in acceleration of the sums secured by this Security Instrument, foreclosure by judicial proceeding and sale of the Property. The notice shall further inform Borrower of the right to reinstate after acceleration and the right to assert in the foreclosure proceeding the non-existence of a default or any other defense of Borrower to acceleration and foreclosure. If the default is not cured on or before the date specified in the notice, Lender at its option may require immediate payment in full of all sums secured by this Security Instrument without further demand and may foreclose this Security Instrument by judicial proceeding. Lender shall be entitled to collect all expenses incurred in pursuing the remedies provided in this paragraph 19, including, but not limited to, reasonable attorneys' fees and costs of title evidence.

20. Lender in Possession. Upon acceleration under paragraph 19 or abandonment of the Property, Lender (by judicially appointed receiver) shall be entitled to enter upon, take possession of and manage the Property and to collect the rents of the Property including those past due. Any rents collected by Lender or the receiver shall be applied first to payment of the costs of management of the Property and collection of rents, including, but not limited to, receiver's fees, premiums on receiver's bonds and reasonable attorneys' fees, and then to the sums secured by this Security Instrument.

21. Release. Upon payment of all sums secured by this Security Instrument, Lender shall release this Security Instrument without charge to Borrower.

22. Waiver of Valuation and Appraisement. Borrower waives all right of valuation and appraisement.

23. Riders to this Security Instrument. If one or more riders are executed by Borrower and recorded together with this Security Instrument, the covenants and agreements of each such rider shall be incorporated into and shall amend and supplement the covenants and agreements of this Security Instrument as if the rider(s) were a part of this Security Instrument. [Check applicable box(es)]

☐ Adjustable Rate Rider   ☐ Condominium Rider   ☐ 2-4 Family Rider

☐ Graduated Payment Rider   ☐ Planned Unit Development Rider

☐ Other(s) [specify]

BY SIGNING BELOW, Borrower accepts and agrees to the terms and covenants contained in this Security Instrument and in any rider(s) executed by Borrower and recorded with it.

....(Seal)
—Borrower

....(Seal)
—Borrower

———————————— [Space Below This Line For Acknowledgment] ————————————

[D1259]

[235]

APPENDIX B

ADJUSTABLE RATE NOTE AND MORTGAGE RIDER FORMS

The Federal National Mortgage Association (FNMA) and the Federal Home Loan Mortgage Corporation (FHLMC) recently developed a uniform Adjustable Rate Note and a uniform Adjustable Rate Rider to the FNMA/FHLMC standard mortgage. The FNMA/FHLMC uniform note and mortgage instruments under which interest may be adjusted every three years are reproduced below. FNMA and FHLMC have also created identical forms providing for interest adjustment at one and five year intervals.

ADJUSTABLE RATE NOTE & RIDER

ADJUSTABLE RATE NOTE
(3 Year Index—Payment Cap)
THIS NOTE CONTAINS PROVISIONS ALLOWING FOR CHANGES IN MY INTEREST RATE AND MY MONTHLY PAYMENT. I MAY LIMIT MY MONTHLY PAYMENT INCREASES TO 7½% EACH YEAR IF THE PROVISIONS OF THIS NOTE PERMIT ME TO DO SO.

.... , 19........ .... , ...
[City]   [State]

....
[Property Address]

1. BORROWER'S PROMISE TO PAY

In return for a loan that I have received, I promise to pay U.S. $ .... (this amount is called "principal"), plus interest, to the order of the Lender. The Lender is ....
....

I understand that the Lender may transfer this Note. The Lender or anyone who takes this Note by transfer and who is entitled to receive payments under this Note is called the "Note Holder."

2. INTEREST

Interest will be charged on unpaid principal until the full amount of principal has been paid. I will pay interest at a yearly rate of .... %. The interest rate I will pay will change in accordance with Section 4 of this Note.

The interest rate required by this Section 2 and Section 4 of this Note is the rate I will pay both before and after any default described in Section 10(B) of this Note.

3. PAYMENTS

(A) Time and Place of Payments

I will pay principal and interest by making payments every month.

I will make my monthly payments on the first day of each month beginning on .... , 19 .... I will make these payments every month until I have paid all of the principal and interest and any other charges described below that I may owe under this Note. My monthly payments will be applied to interest before principal. If, on .... , ... , I still owe amounts under this Note, I will pay those amounts in full on that date, which is called the "maturity date."

I will make my monthly payments at ....
.... or at a different place if required by the Note Holder.

(B) Amount of My Initial Monthly Payments

Each of my initial monthly payments will be in the amount of U.S. $ .... This amount may change.

(C) Monthly Payment Changes

Changes in my monthly payment will reflect changes in the unpaid principal of my loan and in the interest rate that I must pay. The Note Holder will determine my new interest rate and the changed amount of my monthly payment in accordance with Section 4 of this Note.

4. INTEREST RATE AND MONTHLY PAYMENT CHANGES

(A) Change Dates

The interest rate I will pay may change on the first day of .... , 19 .... , and on that day every 36th month thereafter. Each date on which my interest rate could change is called a "Change Date."

(B) The Index

Beginning with the first Change Date, my interest rate will be based on an Index. The "Index" is the weekly average yield on United States Treasury securities adjusted to a constant maturity of 3 years, as made available by the Federal Reserve Board. The most recent Index figure available as of the date 45 days before each Change Date is called the "Current Index."

If the Index is no longer available, the Note Holder will choose a new index which is based upon comparable information. The Note Holder will give me notice of this choice.

(C) Calculation of Changes

Before each Change Date, the Note Holder will calculate my new interest rate by adding ....
.... percentage points (................. %) to the Current Index. The Note Holder will then round the result of this addition to the nearest one-eighth of one percentage point (0.125%). This rounded amount will be my new interest rate until the next Change Date.

MULTISTATE ADJUSTABLE RATE NOTE—3 Year Treasury Index—Single Family—**FNMA/FHLMC Uniform Instrument**   Form 3403 12/83

APPENDIX B

The Note Holder will then determine the amount of the monthly payment that would be sufficient to repay the unpaid principal that I am expected to owe at the Change Date in full on the maturity date at my new interest rate in substantially equal payments. The result of this calculation is called the "Full Payment." It will be the new amount of my monthly payment unless I choose the amount permitted by Section 5 below.

(D) Effective Date of Changes

My new interest rate will become effective on each Change Date. I will pay the amount of my new monthly payment beginning on the first monthly payment date after the Change Date until the amount of my monthly payment changes again.

5. BORROWER'S RIGHT TO LIMIT MONTHLY PAYMENT; REQUIRED FULL PAYMENT

(A) Calculation of Graduated Limited Payment

I may choose to limit the amount of my new monthly payment following a Change Date if my new interest rate would cause the monthly payment I have been paying to increase by more than seven and one-half percent (7.5%). **If I choose to limit the amount of my monthly payment, I must give the Note Holder notice that I am doing so at least 15 days before my first new monthly payment is due.** When I do so, on the first monthly payment date after the Change Date I will begin paying a new monthly payment which will be equal to the amount I have been paying each month for the preceding twelve months multiplied by the number 1.075. Thereafter, on each of the first two anniversaries of my new monthly payment effective date, my monthly payment will again increase to an amount equal to the amount I have been paying each month for the preceding twelve months multiplied by the number 1.075. These amounts are called the "Graduated Limited Payments."

Even if I have chosen to limit my monthly payment, Section 5(B), 5(C) or 5(D) below may require me to pay a different amount.

(B) Reduced Monthly Payment

A Graduated Limited Payment could be greater than the amount of a monthly payment which then would be sufficient to repay my unpaid principal in full on the maturity date at my current interest rate in substantially equal payments. If so, on the date that my paying a Graduated Limited Payment would cause me to pay more than the lower amount, I will instead then begin paying the lower amount as my monthly payment until the next Change Date.

(C) Increased Monthly Payment

My paying a Graduated Limited Payment could cause my unpaid principal to exceed the limit stated in Section 6(B) below. If so, on the date that my paying my monthly payment would cause me to exceed that limit, I will instead begin paying a new monthly payment until the next Change Date. The new monthly payment will be in an amount which would be sufficient to repay my then unpaid principal in full on the maturity date at my current interest rate in substantially equal payments.

(D) Required Full Payment

Beginning with the first monthly payment after the final Change Date, I will pay the Full Payment as my monthly payment.

6. INCREASES IN THE PRINCIPAL AMOUNT TO BE PAID

(A) Additions to My Unpaid Principal

If I choose to pay Graduated Limited Payments, my monthly payment could be less than the amount of the interest portion of the monthly payment that would be sufficient to repay the unpaid principal I owe at the monthly payment date in full on the maturity date in substantially equal payments. If so, each month that the amount of my monthly payment is less than the interest portion, the Note Holder will subtract the amount of my monthly payment from the amount of the interest portion and will add the difference to my unpaid principal. The Note Holder will also add interest on the amount of this difference to my unpaid principal each month. The interest rate on the interest added to principal will be the rate required by Section 4(C) above.

(B) Limit on My Unpaid Principal

My unpaid principal can never exceed a maximum amount equal to one hundred twenty-five percent (125%) of the principal amount I originally borrowed.

7. NOTICE OF CHANGES

The Note Holder will deliver or mail to me a notice of any changes in my interest rate and the amount of my monthly payment before the effective date of any change. The notice will include information required by law to be given me and also the title and telephone number of a person who will answer any question I may have regarding the notice.

8. BORROWER'S RIGHT TO PREPAY

I have the right to make payments of principal at any time before they are due. A payment of principal only is known as a "prepayment." When I make a prepayment, I will tell the Note Holder in writing that I am doing so.

I may make a full prepayment or partial prepayments without paying any prepayment charge. The Note Holder will use all of my prepayments to reduce the amount of principal that I owe under this Note. If I make a partial prepayment, there will be no changes in the due dates of my monthly payments unless the Note Holder agrees in writing to those changes. My partial prepayment may reduce the amount of my monthly payments after the first Change Date following my partial prepayment. However, any reduction due to my partial prepayment may be offset by an interest rate increase.

9. LOAN CHARGES

If a law, which applies to this loan and which sets maximum loan charges, is finally interpreted so that the interest or other loan charges collected or to be collected in connection with this loan exceed the permitted limits, then: (i) any such loan charge shall be reduced by the amount necessary to reduce the charge to the permitted limit; and (ii) any sums already collected from me which exceeded permitted limits will be refunded to me. The Note Holder may choose to make this refund by reducing the principal I owe under this Note or by making a direct payment to me. If a refund reduces principal, the reduction will be treated as a partial prepayment.

ADJUSTABLE RATE NOTE & RIDER

10. BORROWER'S FAILURE TO PAY AS REQUIRED

(A) Late Charges for Overdue Payments

If the Note Holder has not received the full amount of any monthly payment by the end of .... calendar days after the date it is due, I will pay a late charge to the Note Holder. The amount of the charge will be .... % of my overdue payment of principal and interest. I will pay this late charge promptly but only once on each late payment.

(B) Default

If I do not pay the full amount of each monthly payment on the date it is due, I will be in default.

(C) Notice of Default

If I am in default, the Note Holder may send me a written notice telling me that if I do not pay the overdue amount by a certain date, the Note Holder may require me to pay immediately the full amount of principal which has not been paid and all the interest that I owe on that amount. That date must be at least 30 days after the date on which the notice is delivered or mailed to me.

(D) No Waiver By Note Holder

Even if, at a time when I am in default, the Note Holder does not require me to pay immediately in full as described above, the Note Holder will still have the right to do so if I am in default at a later time.

(E) Payment of Note Holder's Costs and Expenses

If the Note Holder has required me to pay immediately in full as described above, the Note Holder will have the right to be paid back by me for all of its costs and expenses in enforcing this Note to the extent not prohibited by applicable law. Those expenses include, for example, reasonable attorneys' fees.

11. GIVING OF NOTICES

Unless applicable law requires a different method, any notice that must be given to me under this Note will be given by delivering it or by mailing it by first class mail to me at the Property Address above or at a different address if I give the Note Holder a notice of my different address.

Any notice that must be given to the Note Holder under this Note will be given by mailing it by first class mail to the Note Holder at the address stated in Section 3(A) above or at a different address if I am given a notice of that different address.

12. OBLIGATIONS OF PERSONS UNDER THIS NOTE

If more than one person signs this Note, each person is fully and personally obligated to keep all of the promises made in this Note, including the promise to pay the full amount owed. Any person who is a guarantor, surety or endorser of this Note is also obligated to do these things. Any person who takes over these obligations, including the obligations of a guarantor, surety or endorser of this Note, is also obligated to keep all of the promises made in this Note. The Note Holder may enforce its rights under this Note against each person individually or against all of us together. This means that any one of us may be required to pay all of the amounts owed under this Note.

13. WAIVERS

I and any other person who has obligations under this Note waive the rights of presentment and notice of dishonor. "Presentment" means the right to require the Note Holder to demand payment of amounts due. "Notice of dishonor" means the right to require the Note Holder to give notice to other persons that amounts due have not been paid.

14. UNIFORM SECURED NOTE

This Note is a uniform instrument with limited variations in some jurisdictions. In addition to the protections given to the Note Holder under this Note, a Mortgage, Deed of Trust or Security Deed (the "Security Instrument"), dated the same date as this Note, protects the Note Holder from possible losses which might result if I do not keep the promises which I make in this Note. That Security Instrument describes how and under what conditions I may be required to make immediate payment in full of all amounts I owe under this Note. Some of those conditions are described as follows:

Transfer of the Property or a Beneficial Interest in Borrower. If all or any part of the Property or any interest in it is sold or transferred (or if a beneficial interest in Borrower is sold or transferred and Borrower is not a natural person) without Lender's prior written consent, Lender may, at its option, require immediate payment in full of all sums secured by this Security Instrument. However, this option shall not be exercised by Lender if exercise is prohibited by federal law as of the date of this Security Instrument. Lender also shall not exercise this option if: (a) Borrower causes to be submitted to Lender information required by Lender to evaluate the intended transferee as if a new loan were being made to the transferee; and (b) Lender reasonably determines that Lender's security will not be impaired by the loan assumption and that the risk of a breach of any covenant or agreement in this Security Instrument is acceptable to Lender.

To the extent permitted by applicable law, Lender may charge a reasonable fee as a condition to Lender's consent to the loan assumption. Lender may also require the transferee to sign an assumption agreement that is acceptable to Lender and that obligates the transferee to keep all the promises and agreements made in the Note and in this Security Instrument. Borrower will continue to be obligated under the Note and this Security Instrument unless Lender releases Borrower in writing.

If Lender exercises the option to require immediate payment in full, Lender shall give Borrower notice of acceleration. The notice shall provide a period of not less than 30 days from the date the notice is delivered or mailed within which Borrower must pay all sums secured by this Security Instrument. If

[*239*]

APPENDIX B

Borrower fails to pay these sums prior to the expiration of this period, Lender may invoke any remedies permitted by this Security Instrument without further notice or demand on Borrower.

WITNESS THE HAND(S) AND SEAL(S) OF THE UNDERSIGNED.

....(Seal)
                                                                                        -Borrower

....(Seal)
                                                                                        -Borrower

....(Seal)
                                                                                        -Borrower

[*Sign Original Only*]

[D1262]

ADJUSTABLE RATE NOTE & RIDER

ADJUSTABLE RATE RIDER
(3 Year Index—Payment Cap)

THIS ADJUSTABLE RATE RIDER is made this .... day of .... , 19 .... , and is incorporated into and shall be deemed to amend and supplement the Mortgage, Deed of Trust or Security Deed (the "Security Instrument") of the same date given by the undersigned (the "Borrower") to secure Borrower's Adjustable Rate Note (the "Note") to ....
.... (the "Lender") of the same date and covering the property described in the Security Instrument and located at:

....
[Property Address]

> **THE NOTE CONTAINS PROVISIONS ALLOWING FOR CHANGES IN THE INTEREST RATE AND THE MONTHLY PAYMENT. THE BORROWER MAY LIMIT MONTHLY PAYMENT INCREASES TO 7½% EACH YEAR IF THE PROVISIONS OF THE NOTE PERMIT IT.**

Additional Covenants. In addition to the covenants and agreements made in the Security Instrument, Borrower and Lender further covenant and agree as follows:

A. INTEREST RATE AND MONTHLY PAYMENT CHANGES

The Note provides for an initial interest rate of .... %. The Note provides for changes in the interest rate and the monthly payments, as follows:

4. INTEREST RATE AND MONTHLY PAYMENT CHANGES

(A) Change Dates

The interest rate I will pay may change on the first day of .... , 19 .... , and on that day every 36th month thereafter. Each date on which my interest rate could change is called a "Change Date."

(B) The Index

Beginning with the first Change Date, my interest rate will be based on an Index. The "Index" is the weekly average yield on United States Treasury securities adjusted to a constant maturity of 3 years, as made available by the Federal Reserve Board. The most recent Index figure available as of the date 45 days before each Change Date is called the "Current Index."

If the Index is no longer available, the Note Holder will choose a new index which is based upon comparable information. The Note Holder will give me notice of this choice.

(C) Calculation of Changes

Before each Change Date, the Note Holder will calculate my new interest rate by adding ....
.... percentage points (.................%) to the Current Index. The Note Holder will then round the result of this addition to the nearest one-eighth of one percentage point (0.125%). This rounded amount will be my new interest rate until the next Change Date.

The Note Holder will then determine the amount of the monthly payment that would be sufficient to repay the unpaid principal that I am expected to owe at the Change Date in full on the maturity date at my new interest rate in substantially equal payments. The result of this calculation is called the "Full Payment." It will be the new amount of my monthly payment unless I choose the amount permitted by Section 5 below.

(D) Effective Date of Changes

My new interest rate will become effective on each Change Date. I will pay the amount of my new monthly payment beginning on the first monthly payment date after the Change Date until the amount of my monthly payment changes again.

5. BORROWER'S RIGHT TO LIMIT MONTHLY PAYMENT; REQUIRED FULL PAYMENT

(A) Calculation of Graduated Limited Payment

I may choose to limit the amount of my new monthly payment following a Change Date if my new interest rate would cause the monthly payment I have been paying to increase by more than seven and one-half percent (7.5%). **If I choose to limit the amount of my monthly payment, I must give the Note Holder notice that I am doing so at least 15 days before my first new monthly payment is due.** When I do so, on the first monthly payment date after the Change Date I will begin paying a new monthly payment which will be equal to the amount I have been paying each month for the preceding twelve months multiplied by the number 1.075. Thereafter, on each of the first two anniversaries of my new monthly payment effective date, my monthly payment will again increase to an amount equal to the amount I have been paying each month for the preceding twelve months multiplied by the number 1.075. These amounts are called the "Graduated Limited Payments."

Even if I have chosen to limit my monthly payment, Section 5(B), 5(C) or 5(D) below may require me to pay a different amount.

MULTISTATE ADJUSTABLE RATE RIDER—3 Year Treasury Index—Single Family—FNMA/FHLMC Uniform Instrument   Form 3103 12/83

APPENDIX B

(B) Reduced Monthly Payment

A Graduated Limited Payment could be greater than the amount of a monthly payment which then would be sufficient to repay my unpaid principal in full on the maturity date at my current interest rate in substantially equal payments. If so, on the date my paying a Graduated Limited Payment would cause me to pay more than the lower amount, I will instead then begin paying the lower amount as my monthly payment until the next Change Date.

(C) Increased Monthly Payment

My paying a Graduated Limited Payment could cause my unpaid principal to exceed the limit stated in Section 6(B) below. If so, on the date that my paying my monthly payment would cause me to exceed that limit, I will instead begin paying a new monthly payment until the next Change Date. The new monthly payment will be in an amount which would be sufficient to repay my then unpaid principal in full on the maturity date at my current interest rate in substantially equal payments.

(D) Required Full Payment

Beginning with the first monthly payment after the final Change Date, I will pay the Full Payment as my monthly payment.

6. INCREASES IN THE PRINCIPAL AMOUNT TO BE PAID

(A) Additions to My Unpaid Principal

If I choose to pay Graduated Limited Payments, my monthly payment could be less than the amount of the interest portion of the monthly payment that would be sufficient to repay the unpaid principal I owe at the monthly payment date in full on the maturity date in substantially equal payments. If so, each month that the amount of my monthly payment is less than the interest portion, the Note Holder will subtract the amount of my monthly payment from the amount of the interest portion and will add the difference to my unpaid principal. The Note Holder will also add interest on the amount of this difference to my unpaid principal each month. The interest rate on the interest added to principal will be the rate required by Section 4(C) above.

(B) Limit on My Unpaid Principal

My unpaid principal can never exceed a maximum amount equal to one hundred twenty-five percent (125%) of the principal amount I originally borrowed.

7. NOTICE OF CHANGES

The Note Holder will deliver or mail to me a notice of any changes in my interest rate and the amount of my monthly payment before the effective date of any change. The notice will include information required by law to be given me and also the title and telephone number of a person who will answer any question I may have regarding the notice.

B. TRANSFER OF THE PROPERTY OR A BENEFICIAL INTEREST IN BORROWER

Uniform Covenant 17 of the Security Instrument is amended to read as follows:

Transfer of the Property or a Beneficial Interest in Borrower. If all or any part of the Property or any interest in it is sold or transferred (or if a beneficial interest in Borrower is sold or transferred and Borrower is not a natural person) without Lender's prior written consent, Lender may, at its option, require immediate payment in full of all sums secured by this Security Instrument. However, this option shall not be exercised by Lender if exercise is prohibited by federal law as of the date of this Security Instrument. Lender also shall not exercise this option if: (a) Borrower causes to be submitted to Lender information required by Lender to evaluate the intended transferee as if a new loan were being made to the transferee; and (b) Lender reasonably determines that Lender's security will not be impaired by the loan assumption and that the risk of a breach of any covenant or agreement in this Security Instrument is acceptable to Lender.

To the extent permitted by applicable law, Lender may charge a reasonable fee as a condition to Lender's consent to the loan assumption. Lender may also require the transferee to sign an assumption agreement that is acceptable to Lender and that obligates the transferee to keep all the promises and agreements made in the Note and in this Security Instrument. Borrower will continue to be obligated under the Note and this Security Instrument unless Lender releases Borrower in writing.

If Lender exercises the option to require immediate payment in full, Lender shall give Borrower notice of acceleration. The notice shall provide a period of not less than 30 days from the date the notice is delivered or mailed within which Borrower must pay all sums secured by this Security Instrument. If Borrower fails to pay these sums prior to the expiration of this period, Lender may invoke any remedies permitted by this Security Instrument without further notice or demand on Borrower.

BY SIGNING BELOW, Borrower accepts and agrees to the terms and covenants contained in this Adjustable Rate Rider.

....(Seal)
                                                                                            -Borrower

....(Seal)
                                                                                            -Borrower

APPENDIX C
CONDOMINIUM RIDER

The Federal National Mortgage Association and the Federal Home Loan Mortgage Corporation have created a Condominium Rider to their standard mortgage instrument. It is reproduced below.

APPENDIX C

CONDOMINIUM RIDER

THIS CONDOMINIUM RIDER is made this .... day of ...., 19........., and is incorporated into and shall be deemed to amend and supplement the Mortgage, Deed of Trust or Security Deed (the "Security Instrument") of the same date given by the undersigned (the "Borrower") to secure Borrower's Note to .... (the "Lender") of the same date and covering the Property described in the Security Instrument and located at:

....
[Property Address]

The Property includes a unit in, together with an undivided interest in the common elements of, a condominium project known as:

....
[Name of Condominium Project]

(the "Condominium Project"). If the owners association or other entity which acts for the Condominium Project (the "Owners Association") holds title to property for the benefit or use of its members or shareholders, the Property also includes Borrower's interest in the Owners Association and the uses, proceeds and benefits of Borrower's interest.

CONDOMINIUM COVENANTS. In addition to the covenants and agreements made in the Security Instrument, Borrower and Lender further covenant and agree as follows:

A. Condominium Obligations. Borrower shall perform all of Borrower's obligations under the Condominium Project's Constituent Documents. The "Constituent Documents" are the: (i) Declaration or any other document which creates the Condominium Project; (ii) by-laws; (iii) code of regulations; and (iv) other equivalent documents. Borrower shall promptly pay, when due, all dues and assessments imposed pursuant to the Constituent Documents.

B. Hazard Insurance. So long as the Owners Association maintains, with a generally accepted insurance carrier, a "master" or "blanket" policy on the Condominium Project which is satisfactory to Lender and which provides insurance coverage in the amounts, for the periods, and against the hazards Lender requires, including fire and hazards included within the term "extended coverage," then:

(i) Lender waives the provision in Uniform Covenant 2 for the monthly payment to Lender of one-twelfth of the yearly premium installments for hazard insurance on the Property; and

(ii) Borrower's obligation under Uniform Covenant 5 to maintain hazard insurance coverage on the Property is deemed satisfied to the extent that the required coverage is provided by the Owners Association policy.

Borrower shall give Lender prompt notice of any lapse in required hazard insurance coverage.

In the event of a distribution of hazard insurance proceeds in lieu of restoration or repair following a loss to the Property, whether to the unit or to common elements, any proceeds payable to Borrower are hereby assigned and shall be paid to Lender for application to the sums secured by the Security Instrument, with any excess paid to Borrower.

C. Public Liability Insurance. Borrower shall take such actions as may be reasonable to insure that the Owners Association maintains a public liability insurance policy acceptable in form, amount, and extent of coverage to Lender.

D. Condemnation. The proceeds of any award or claim for damages, direct or consequential, payable to Borrower in connection with any condemnation or other taking of all or any part of the Property, whether of the unit or of the common elements, or for any conveyance in lieu of condemnation, are hereby assigned and shall be paid to Lender. Such proceeds shall be applied by Lender to the sums secured by the Security Instrument as provided in Uniform Covenant 9.

E. Lender's Prior Consent. Borrower shall not, except after notice to Lender and with Lender's prior written consent, either partition or subdivide the Property or consent to:

(i) the abandonment or termination of the Condominium Project, except for abandonment or termination required by law in the case of substantial destruction by fire or other casualty or in the case of a taking by condemnation or eminent domain;

(ii) any amendment to any provision of the Constituent Documents if the provision is for the express benefit of Lender;

(iii) termination of professional management and assumption of self-management of the Owners Association; or

(iv) any action which would have the effect of rendering the public liability insurance coverage maintained by the Owners Association unacceptable to Lender.

F. Remedies. If Borrower does not pay condominium dues and assessments when due, then Lender may pay them. Any amounts disbursed by Lender under this paragraph F shall become additional debt of Borrower secured by the Security Instrument. Unless Borrower and Lender agree to other terms of payment, these amounts shall bear interest from the date of disbursement at the Note rate and shall be payable, with interest, upon notice from Lender to Borrower requesting payment.

BY SIGNING BELOW, Borrower accepts and agrees to the terms and provisions contained in this Condominium Rider.

....(Seal)
                                                                                    Borrower

....(Seal)
                                                                                    Borrower
                                                                                    [D1264]

MULTISTATE CONDOMINIUM RIDER—Single Family—**FNMA/FHLMC UNIFORM INSTRUMENT**   Form 3140 12/83

INDEX

References are to Pages

[*245*]

INDEX
References are to Pages

[247]

INDEX
References are to Pages

[*254*]

[*256*]

INDEX
References are to Pages